*When
Your
Parents
Need You*

When Your Parents Need You

A Caregiver's Guide

by RITA ROBINSON

IBS PRESS
Santa Monica, CA

Cover and book design by Melvin L. Harris and Susan Muller-Harris
Type composition by Susan Muller-Harris
Copyediting by Laura Norvig and Miriam Jacobson

IBS PRESS
744 Pier Avenue
Santa Monica, CA 90405
(213)450-6485

IBS PRESS FIRST PRINTING, MARCH 1990

Library of Congress Cataloging-in-Publication Data
Robinson, Rita.
When your parents need you : a caregiver's guide / by Rita
Robinson.
p. cm.
Includes bibliographical references.
ISBN 1-877880-01-9 : $9.95
1. Parents, Aged—Care—United States. 2. Adult children—
United States—Family relationships. 3. Caregivers—United States—
Psychology. 4. Aged—Services for—United States. I. Title.
HQ1063.6.R63 1990
649.8—dc20   90-4138
                                                                  CIP

ISBN 1-877880-01-9

Manufactured in the United States of America

Dedication

for my sister,
Theda Lambert,
one tough lady

Acknowledgments

My thanks to the staff at *IBS Press*, who are dedicated to presenting books that will help people in times of turmoil.

My gratitude to the many people, professionals and family members, who helped make this book possible by sharing their knowledge and feelings with me. They are:

Joseph Becker, Peter Braun, Harold Bloomfield, Dana Brookins, Sheila Bunting, James Callahan Jr., Russell Coile, Joyce Colony, Connie Courtney, Linda and Bob Falconer, Maria Fiatarone, Kamiko Ford, Lynn Goldis, Catherine Goodman, Vernon Greene, Anne Griffin, Marc Hankin, Nancy Hardy, Robert Henkin, Russell Hereford, Leach Hernandez, David Holmes, Charlotte Humphris, Tia Kudish, Theda and Leslie Lambert, Richard Lindsay, Carolyn Lindgren, Beverly Looper, Stephen McConnell, Paula Morris, Nell Noddings, Carolyn Nolan, Andrea Obston, Jon Pynoos, Angela Rosenberg, Susan Schiffman, Sister Margaret Mary, Burke Stinson, Dick Teeling, Maurice Thompson, Peter Vitaliano, Carol Vogel, Patricia Jo Wilkinson, Patty Wyborny, Barbara Wilson, Bradley Williams, and many unnamed people who, in casual conversation, told me their stories concerning the care of elderly parents.

Contents

Foreword

THERE IS A TWILIGHT ZONE between life as we know it and death. It's a period of time when your mind is not quite here, a part of your life that typically rears its head when you age. Your memory fails, your judgment becomes less rational and your body starts to lose the ability to do what your head tells it to do.

Historically, this twilight zone was not a societal problem. Elderly enfeebled people did not live long once they entered this zone. Rumor has it, the Eskimos sent their dying elders out onto the ice, and the American Indians sent theirs into the forest to die.

But modern science has changed the picture. Through the marvels of medicine we are now able to keep people alive for much longer periods than were previously considered possible. People in their early sixties are no longer considered elderly. If we become ill and enfeebled, demented and even paralyzed from head to foot, science can keep us alive for a long time.

Admittedly, they still have trouble keeping the brain functional. The rest of the body, oh my, they can keep that going for years! Remember Karen Quinlan? Her body "lived" for over fifteen years after she was determined brain dead. We no longer have the luxury of expecting our demise to be a short process.

❤   ❤   ❤

When I was a child, we lived in a three-family house. My family lived in a flat on the third floor. My mother's brother and his wife and kids lived on the first floor, and my mother's parents lived in the middle flat. If one person was ill, we could all share the burden of providing care because we all lived together.

Not anymore. It takes me forty-five minutes to an hour each way to visit my mother or my siblings, even though we all live in the same area (Los Angeles). I am a lawyer and my work requires long hours. My wife is a professional who works. We need both incomes, and it simply is not possible for either of us to travel an hour and a half every day to check in on my mother and see if she is OK. Many people like us cannot provide the care for their parents themselves, and finding out what is available is often a Kafkaesque nightmare leading nowhere.

When my mother deteriorates and needs custodial care, we will have to hire someone. My mother wants to remain in her own home, which will be expensive.

Professional home care often costs as much as a nursing home or more. A few years of high-tech home care could exhaust her savings. Medicaid would kick in then, and pay for her care. But, knowing my mother, if she were to exhaust all her savings and have nothing left to leave to her children, she would probably lose the will to live and die from depression.

Somehow, the process of aging in America does not seem to be getting kinder and gentler. More and more con artists prey on the aged, stealing their homes and savings from them, cutting them off from their families and extracting wills, thus disinheriting the people who really cared for them. When we sue the abusers, they hire lawyers of their own and fight vigorous battles to protect their ill-gotten gains. California's State Senator, Herschel Rosenthal, is fighting hard for the enactment of a bill I drafted for him to protect the elderly, called the Elder Abuse Civil Protection Act. It would make the abusers pay for the legal fees required for the recovery of property stolen from the elderly. But the act has not been adopted yet and the abuse goes on. No matter how vigilant we are, many of us learn to our horror that our parents have been abused by evil-doers who somehow found their way into our parents lives when we were away at work.

Access to medical care is a severe problem for our parents. Aged people often lose the capacity to understand their need for medical treatment and sometimes reject it when they need it most. Many stroke victims need a conservator appointed in order to have someone who can consent to medical treatment, even though the confused stroke victim may think that he or she does not need medical attention. Many of us not only must battle with a confused and frightened parent to get conservatorship, but also fight a judicial system that is so overly focused on preserving the elder's rights it neglects to preserve their well-being.

Although most health care providers honestly try to provide good care to the aged, many bad apples overly economize, and neglect their patients. I have personally fought with hospitals that tried to dump patients after they ran out of Medicare benefits. It is possible to stop the abuse, but the fight can be costly from both the emotional and financial standpoint.

Governmental agencies charged with the responsibility of providing medical and social services often provide misleading advice and take forever to grant benefits, or deny benefits to people who are entitled to them. Private agencies dispensing services to the elderly tend to be either disorganized or hard to find.

Spouses of the disabled and enfeebled elderly must wind their way through a morass to avoid impoverishment. Admittedly, it is no longer necessary for the spouse of a catastrophically ill person to lose everything. In 1988, Congress passed a federal version of a 1984 California law that I drafted to prevent spousal impoverishment. Poverty can be avoided, but you need the skill of a lawyer to do so. Estate planning is no longer the domain only of the wealthy. Middle class and poor people must now hire lawyers to devise complicated plans to protect their rights under the Medicaid and related insurance programs. We should be able to get our benefits without so much hassle.

We, the survivors, must live on, suffering through that sense of continuous loss as our parent is dying, and experiencing all the related problems of providing care on the way down. We ask ourselves where we went wrong, how we have let our loved one down, what we should have done. No one seems able to help. It is a wonder that there is not more elder abuse simply due to the caregiver's frustration at being powerless and overwhelmed.

Finally, there is some help from someone who cares, and who knows about caring for aging parents from both a professional and a personal perspective. This book dispels the myths. It tells you what traps to avoid, and what to look out for. It shows you how to help yourself find your way when your parents enter the twilight zone.

I was honored when Rita Robinson asked me to write this introduction. She is one of the most impressive clients I have ever had. When I met Rita, her father was dying from multiple stroke syndrome, and her mother, who was suffering from Alzheimer's disease, was making attempts to commit suicide. At the same time, her parents ran out of money to pay for hospital and custodial care, and when Rita applied for Medicaid and In-Home Supportive Services, the local Medicaid office accused her and her sister of everything short of fraud. They denied benefits and ignored the proof of eligibility we sent them. They refused to take our calls and hung up on us. But through it all, Rita remained rational and calm, doing what had to be done, avoiding hysteria, doing the work of three people, and crying only when it wouldn't interfere with her doing what was necessary.

This book will help many people take those steps that can prevent unnecessary impoverishment and improper care. It will enable adult children to find the help that they and their parents need; it will enable them to minimize their own suffering and to more easily live with the aftermath of their parent's decline. It will help these caregivers find their own way back to life.

Rita has made a valuable contribution to the field within these pages, and I recommend this book for everyone. Even if your parents do not slowly deteriorate, the ideas explored in this book will expand your awareness and enable you to plan for your own old age.

MARC HANKIN
February, 1990

Lawyer & Elder Care Advocate
Fulbright & Jaworski
Los Angeles, California

Author, Elder Abuse Civil
Protection Act (Senate Bill #851)
and Spousal Impoverishment
Protection legislation

Prologue

Nov. 3, 1989

Dear Dana,

I always write the date now to remind me of what day it is. Taking on the responsibility of my parents' care is like getting sucked into a black hole. Dick and Bev really saved the entire situation. With their help, we got Mama on In-Home Supportive Services and we hope to do the same with Daddy.

Like it or not, this, for now is all-consuming. One of the doctors finally returned my call, and the word is: Daddy won't get better. It's a matter of time—a short time. So, we're going to bring him home to die and to do that we have to physically take him from the nursing home ourselves. D-day is Tuesday and my son, Doss, and Theda's son are going to help. The nursing home doesn't want to let go. The doctors and the nursing home are paid by **Medi-Cal*** and they want to keep Daddy for the bucks. Ironically, we had to fight to get him the proper care in a hospital and now we have to fight to get him out. Through In-Home Supportive Services he will get the same quality of care, and the state will pay for it.

I told the administrator at the hospital what I'm going to do and at first she threatened me, saying, "You can't take his medication with you. That's ours." Then she said I would have to sign something and take responsibility for Dad's death. When I went down to visit Daddy that evening, I confronted her. I had already checked on my rights and, indeed, they must give me the name of the medication or turn it over to another physician. I don't have to sign diddly squat, and it's state law that we can take him home for his care. The administrator started backing down.

It was only after I talked to her that the doctor finally called and leveled with me about my dad's condition. He's actually mailing me the papers to give to the hospital so no extraordinary measures will be taken if he goes back in there, which he won't unless he has another stroke before Tuesday when I bring them the papers. If I don't get those papers signed properly, by state law he would be put on life-support machines and could linger indefinitely in a comatose state.

With both of my parents out of commission, it's been nearly impossible to get stuff done. Mama is a mess to care for. It isn't just a simple matter of being there with her and her being this nice sweet lady I once knew.

*Terms appearing in bold italics are defined in Chapter 8, "Who Pays?"

She gets violent because she's so confused with Daddy not there. My sister, Theda, had her for three days and had to put her on tranquilizers. We can't get her to bathe—nothing. There is relief now, however, with the in-home caregiver and I'm finally able to go home for a few days.

It's not a simple matter at all. You don't just decide, "Well, we'll do this. It's best for all of us." You have to work through the "system" which is cumbersome and reveals health care in America at its worst. Most of the days I'm OK. But the anger doesn't go away. Yesterday—my first day home in awhile—I cried on and off. I'm dealing with such conflicting emotions.

When I take Mama to the hospital to see Daddy, she literally runs in and tries to sit in his lap in the wheel chair. I get her sitting on the bed and Daddy flaps his feet in the chair and moves as close to her as possible. He's trying to smile and he's teary. She asks why he can't talk. I tell her. She kisses his hand, his tears.

"I'll take care of you," she says.

He slowly utters, "I l o v e ..." and drops his head.

He pats her hand with the left hand he can move and then suddenly he looks at us and I know the light has gone off again for a minute or two. Who are you people? his eyes seem to say. He drops his head, rests a minute, looks up and then, he knows us again and he laughs at my jokes. He recognizes us. Mama and Daddy start back billing and cooing, and I leave the room so I won't cry in front of them.

Then there are times when Mama is beating the table top telling us to go away and threatening suicide. We removed the gun Daddy had in his bedside drawer and we know there's another in the house, but we can't find it.

We had to clean out a room for the full-time caregiver and what we found was incredible. Twelve or more big plastic sacks of junk and trash to throw out. We had to cart the stuff over to a neighbors because Mama was starting to go through the trash.

We got a neighbor to move the RV off the premises so we can sell it to help start paying off some of Daddy's bills. Daddy has never been able to handle money —that's why we were so poor and in debt when I was a kid. I remember one time eating spaghetti with ketchup over it for two days because we had no money. So, I start dealing with some resentments. Then I switch back and think of this loving, gentle, good humored man who's dying a few miles away in the hospital, and whose wife is going to continually ask, "Where's Bobby? I want Bobby." And then I go over and hold her and she's soft and gentle and clings to me.

Well, this whole thing is the death of many things and that's life.

Love, Rita

❤   ❤   ❤

Nov. 10, 1989

DEAR PAUL,

Everything that's happened previously in my life was a rehearsal for what's going on now. And before I fill you in on some of it, believe me, you've been a good teacher.

As I mentioned before, Mom has Alzheimer's and Dad was taking care of her. Well, he had a stroke three weeks ago. We battled with the hospital to not release him to her, and later, battled with the convalescent care hospital they sent him to for therapy and where he suffered a second stroke, to get him out. After dealing with all that and then the bureaucracy to get the both of them on **Medi-Cal** so that they could have in-home care and stay together, I'm numb. But I'm also happy and I know the numbness will pass.

There was so much to handle and so many conflicting emotions, that I welcomed my periods of insanity while I was working my way through the maze. It was all my sister and I could handle to keep each other calm, and keep the sun shining in. I've had to wipe my dad's butt which didn't bother me at all but which I know was humiliating to him; danced around the room with a box of sugar-coated cereal to my dad's delight who loves the stuff and wasn't given any in the hospital; cried until I thought my eyes would never be the same again; and raged at the inadequacy of the health care system.

I've pretty well handled the grief with my mother. She is simply not the person I once knew and she can't help it. Today she attempted suicide (slashed her wrists and required stitches) because she didn't like the caregiver in the home (she doesn't like my sister or I at times, nor my dad, and wants us all to leave her alone). She's really quite bonkers. The psychiatric hospital where she was admitted, finally put her on a seventy-two-hour hold and then maybe, if we're lucky, they'll keep her another two weeks. We are just in the process of getting both my parents into the system. They don't have their **Medi-Cal** numbers yet, but the interview is done and most of the paperwork. I'm not going to go into how happy the institutions are to deal with someone who doesn't have their number yet.

So that's what's been going on. Actually, the suicide attempt today didn't faze me much. I'm home in the mountains handling everything by phone. I advised my sister and the neighbors who took her to the hospital not to take her home if the hospital asked them to. Yeah, I've learned how to deal with the system. The same way I did when I pushed my dad in his wheelchair out of the convalescent hospital with the administrator saying I had to sign the papers, which I didn't. I just giggled as the administrator thrust the paper in my face while I pushed Daddy out to the car.

The thing is, through it all, I have no animosity toward anyone. I feel sorry for the doctors, the administrators—the people who are forced to work in this rotten system of care in this country.

The doctor says Dad is due to have another stroke anytime, and good—let the poor man die at home in his bed with his cats. He's aware of everything going on and laughs at every joke and silly antic I pull.

Isn't it ironic that the book I'm now working on is titled, *When Your Parents Need You?* After Dad had the first stroke I got a week's extension on my deadline. After his second stroke, and now the suicide attempt, well, the stress of both responsibilities is wearing me down, but at least I can add an account of my own experiences to the book.

I've tapped some of the sources and people I wrote about to keep me out of the loony bin myself. Until you've been through it, you can't imagine the red tape. It kills you. And on top of that, so many of the people you're dealing with are so hardened to the system and overworked, that they don't give a damn. You are less than a number, and they don't even want to give you that.

I have now been through everything I wrote about —all the stories others told me—and then some. The neurologist who examined Dad in the hospital never did return my sister's or my calls. My daughter happened to see the neurologist when she was visiting Daddy in the hospital and he said, "Well, it looks like your grandfather will be pretty much OK after some therapy." Well, that was before the second stroke.

Dad's primary care physician (who directs all these other doctors), sent forms to fill out so that Daddy won't be kept alive by extraordinary measures. How funny. Daddy has to sign them. He can't even talk. He understands you, and that's about it. We have to work through an attorney to get conservatorship so that our signatures will do. If we're lucky, he'll die at home in bed in his own surroundings carrying with him the memories of a happier time.

Each time I feel like I'm going bonkers over this stuff, I tell myself that "this too shall pass" and I know it will. Today, as soon as I did what I could by phone with the emergency ward on my mom's suicide attempt, I went for a two-hour walk in the national forest up here, which is only three blocks from my house. I love it up here so much that it nearly overwhelms me sometimes. Even driving down to my folks, usually to face something horrible, I drive through areas of the most incredible fall colors imaginable—miles and miles of oranges, yellows, reds and golds mixed in among the solid green of the pines. One day while driving down, the wind kicked up and sent such a flurry of colored leaves across the road that I had to slow down. I love the trails, the little shops, having everything so handy yet being away from it all, and I love my home.

During the walk in the woods, I chanced upon my good old friends—the horses. It's been a long time since I'd seen them, but they remembered me. The black one with the devilish eyes prancing at my side, the white, wide-rumped earth mama nudging me in the back, and the semi-wild red one a short distance behind. It was a joy to see them in my circle of energy again.

Well, I'll leave you on that happy note. I know in my heart there are better times around the corner—I'm just groping to find the corner.

Love, Rita.

Introduction

WHEN I BEGAN THIS BOOK in 1989, I had no idea that by the time it neared completion my life would have changed so dramatically, along with some of my thoughts on caregiving. In the beginning, my father, who was a seventy-seven-year-old vibrant aging gentleman, was caring for my mother who had Alzheimer's. Her disease, which had been progressing slowly up until that point, had altered the family's life spiritually, emotionally and physically, but we kept things going pretty much as usual. The families—my sister's and mine—have always spent Thanksgiving and Easter at my parents' place. For the past few years, because of Mom's condition, we did all the planning and supplied food for the feasts. We each live about a two-hour's drive from their mobile home which sits on a hilltop overlooking the lake at Elsinore, California.

Daddy reveled in all of it and pleaded with us to keep it up. No, it wasn't too much on him and Mama, he said. We visited as frequently as our schedules would allow: I'm single and support myself, and my sister, who was diagnosed last year with multiple sclerosis, has a costume-making business. All in all, we're pretty normal people. Those who are helping their aged parents don't come in specially wrapped packages. Most of us are struggling with our own lives—dealing with day-to-day problems of paying bills, taking care of children, health problems, relationships, marriages and divorces, and aging. We fumble and do our best.

We tried to relieve Daddy when we could from his constant supervision of Mom. He played the drums in a band and sometimes I would drive down so he could have a "night out with the boys" after playing a gig. The truth is, though, we all have our own lives, commitments and responsibilities. He took the brunt of the care of Mama. All that changed on October 19, 1989, one month before this book was due, and after I had already interviewed dozens of researchers, gerontologists, physicians and families involved with the care of the aged in the United States.

Daddy suffered one stroke and then another. We were thrown into the health care "system." The system is mentioned frequently in this book by other caregivers and professionals involved with the problems of caring for the aged in the United States. The system is twofold. At times it's like a lumpy, bumpy mattress, and at other times it turns into a bed of pointy needles. The system varies in every state. There is no easy access into it, thus, it's cumbersome and draining to use. It will push you to frustration. It is the mattress losing its stuffing. And then, just as suddenly, it might comfort you.

All the caregivers I interviewed for this book helped provide me with the strength I needed to continue to help my parents finish out their lives in dignity, and for me to get on with my own life.

Caregiving is not just hands-on-care, bureaucracies and paper work. It involves every type of emotion imaginable. Sometimes I feel as if the paperwork and problems will never end, and other days, it seems my life might return to normal. My sister and I have decided that it balances out pretty well. We seem to get one good day, and then one bad day. But I'm an optimist and believe that eventually, the good days will far outnumber the bad ones. I have this optimism because I've listened to other caregivers.

❤   ❤   ❤

1987

Two women were standing at the counter with me at a print shop. One was tall, well-groomed and had a smile on her face, but she sighed heavily as if the waiting were bothersome. She clearly had a job to get back to and was annoyed at the interruption. The other woman's hands shook as she tried to pat her dishevelled hair into place and straighten her crumpled blouse. She shifted from one foot to the other.

We joked about how no matter where you go, there is a line to wait in. The first woman said she had to get back to the office in a hurry, and the second said she had to hurry home to her mother who was suffering from Alzheimer's and who would drive her husband crazy if she didn't return soon. While she bit her lip nervously I said, "Oh, isn't that ironic. I'm here to get some copies of this article on Alzheimer's to send to my sister. My mother was just diagnosed with it."

The distraught woman turned to me and nearly in tears said, "I'm so sorry for you. I've been taking care of my mother for three years and it's awful. My marriage is falling apart, I'm sick all the time, I've had to give up all my outside activities...I don't know what I'm going to do. Mom can stay awake for twenty-four hours at a time. She paces back and forth. Throws her food. Won't take her medication. I'm just about at the end of my rope."

A chill passed through my body as I thought of my mother. She was just in the beginning stages of the disease and simply sat quietly with a sad expression on her face. Her deep brown eyes which once sparkled, were now deadened. She spoke very little, and when she did, it was usually something about the past. Occasionally, she would become irritated and lash out at my dad, my sister and me—something I'd never seen her do before. My parents are gentle people and only once when I was grown and married had I heard her utter a "damn." When she raged and slammed the door now, it shook up all of us.

The thought crossed my mind, Oh my God. Is this what I have to look forward to?

The other woman turned to us and said, "You may find this hard to believe, but my mother just died. She too had Alzheimer's. It was sad...but..." She paused, looked at the other woman standing next to me, and clammed up.

As I left, the woman whose mother had died followed me out to the car and said, "You don't have to become like that other woman in there. There are things you can do. There is help available. It was a struggle at first, but once I began standing up for my rights—with my mother, my family, the system—it became easier. Neither my mother nor I had to lose our dignity. Please keep that in mind as you go through this."

That's the last I saw of either woman, but the picture of them has flashed through my mind during the past four years as my mother has gotten further into her disease. I'm reminded by those two women that it is up to me to make my life as normal and stable as I possibly can, and to not be swept up in the problems and confusion that surround my parents' illnesses.

As our parents age, we're likely to move into areas that we had never planned to enter, both physically and mentally. Unless we face certain issues honestly and learn to ask for help, I suspect we'll end up like the woman in the print shop who had allowed her spirit to be broken. I've discovered through my own experience and through interviews with those who have been thrust into this role, that it takes a certain amount of toughness and even selfishness to stay on top of this thing that enters our lives without permission.

Although in the back of our minds, hidden in places that are uncomfortable to tap, we know that our parents and other older loved ones are going to age and, perhaps, need care, we don't think much about it until the time comes. Many older Americans stay vital throughout their lives, needing little assistance, but the majority eventually require some sort of help, ranging from minimal to extensive. Some elderly become fragile and simply in need of our support.

Although we tend to think that a large portion of the elderly are placed in convalescent homes, they are a minority. It's estimated that American families provide more than eighty percent of the personal care, home maintenance, shopping and transportation services needed by their elderly relatives.

Once we acknowledge the normal processes taking place with our older relatives, we have a choice: we can provide what is necessary with love and understanding, or we can become bitter and disenchanted. I have experienced emotions from rage to the depth of despair, but I try to stay positive. I want to come out of it at the other end a more knowledgeable, experienced and compassionate person. I also want to stay as healthy as I can during the trip. Whatever attitude we decide to take, the fact remains that the majority of us will help care for our aging parents and relatives in some capacity.

Sheila Bunting of Wayne State University in Michigan, points out that nearly half of the caregivers in the country have been providing care for their aging parents for one to four years and that twenty percent of them have been doing it for more than five years. Nearly eighty percent of them have been providing care seven days a week for an average of four hours a day.

These caregivers experience an enormous amount of stress that isn't wholly understood by other family members or society as a whole, Bunting says. Because there has been little attention paid to caregivers, they have received little support or help for themselves. Additionally, those around them fail to understand the nature of the elderly person's condition.

As an example, I once had to call a neighbor of my mom and dad's about two weeks after Dad had his stroke and when we'd finally managed to get a full-time in-home caregiver for Mom. The neighbor was trying to be nice, but at the same time quiz me as to why Mom needed someone there all the time and why we were taking so many precautions with her smoking habit.

Mom had resumed smoking only recently after abstaining nearly thirty years. Because of her illness, she left burning cigarettes lying around the house. It was just too much to expect the live-in to deal with this practice, especially since my father was coming home from the convalescent hospital within the week, so we let her have them only when one of us or the caregiver had time to sit with her while she smoked. At first she would sneak out to the neighbors and beg them, even talking them into buying her a pack. They simply didn't understand her true condition, (which is true of those who have no knowledge of Alzheimer's), and thought we were being harsh on her. Those who aren't around the person all the time might perceive them as being quite normal, if only a little forgetful. The reality of the disease is far from that. Dad had covered up for, and hidden the disease from, most of the neighbors and many of our relatives. When I called the neighbors to explain the situation, you could tell by the tone of their voices that some of them didn't understand and would never believe that that sweet, gentle woman living next door, or across the street, could get quite violent, demanding, severely depressed and disoriented to the point that she didn't know us.

I try to avoid explaining my mother's condition so that people, somehow, won't think bad of me. When I find myself doing that, I stop myself short. Basically, I don't care what others think as long as in my heart I know I'm doing the best I can.

I'm also not interested in martyrdom. Taking care of an older person is not a pay back for the care our parents gave us when we were infants. The people we'll be caring for aren't babies. They are grown adults who, given the age of today's older population, have been through a world-wide depression, two World Wars (with the threat of a nuclear one forever hanging overhead) and several political bombs such as Watergate.

They have seen hemlines go from the ankles, to the knees to the thighs and back down again. Some have seen horse-drawn carriages and men land on the moon. Many have heard thousands of political promises, and seen many of them broken. They've moved from the farm to the industrialized city to the space age and have still kept the faith, kept a sense of humor and the ability to fight when necessary. They've traveled from an age of innocence to a time when "letting it all hang out," was taken literally.

So when we step into the role of "caregiver," it's almost laughable for us to set ourselves up as the prime source of their existence. To establish ourselves as saviors of our parents, diminishes us and them.

I also refuse to allow others to make me feel guilty about not providing the care for my mom myself. I work full time. I'm not objective about my mother. I hug her and love her and rub her head, and wish I could take away her pain and confusion, but she requires twenty-four-hour supervision.

Some families are able to provide constant care. Others act as managers. Many live thousands of miles from their parents and must help from vast distances.

We hope to be able to keep my parents in their own home with a full-time caregiver for as long as possible. Since my father's stroke, we have managed their entire household from paying bills to buying groceries.

However you decide to handle your parents' care, it is important to keep in mind that we are not our brother's (or sister's) keeper when we give care. We are helpers and we're not alone while treading through this new territory. Many have gone before us and they can help us with the wisdom they have gained from their own experiences.

This book contains interviews with professionals in the field of caregiving, and I've included the latest information from researchers, physicians, mental health experts and caregiving agencies. But it is the nonprofessional caregivers who can offer the greatest advice. They tell of their successes and failures. How they have dealt with the person for whom they were caring, how they came to terms with other family members, the public, doctors, social agencies, spouses, their children and their own fears.

When we begin dealing with our elderly parents on a different level than before—when we come to terms with the fact that they aren't the same father and mother of our childhood and young adulthood, we start coming to terms with the fear of our own mortality. Many of us step into the role of caregiving during our own age crisis, a transition I hadn't acknowledged until my own parents needed me.

When I turned fifty-one, it dawned on me that my parents weren't always going to be around. Somehow, turning thirty and then forty hadn't affected me at all. I was too busy. But this was different. Perhaps I would have touched bases with the aging process even if my parents hadn't reached a point that made me take a different look at our relationship, but I doubt it would have been driven home so effectively.

The truth is, all of the changes we are undergoing are entwined with the internal and external demands we feel concerning our aging parents. Our parents are dealing with their own newfound emotions and feelings at this time, too. We see them growing old, and it forces us to look at ourselves—also growing old.

When
Your
Parents
Need You

The Caregiving Experience 1

IF ANY OF THE FOLLOWING sentences describe you, you have become a caregiver for your parent (or parents):

- ❤ You worry about your parent being left alone at home.
- ❤ Your parent needs help preparing a complete meal and keeping the house straightened.
- ❤ Your parents ignore personal hygiene if you don't remind them.
- ❤ You're in contact with your parent's physician.
- ❤ You perform tasks such as simple gardening and yard work that your parent once took care of.
- ❤ Your parent needs your services for transportation and scheduled activities.

And if these next sentences also describe you, caregiving is having a significant impact on your life:

- You are taking time off from your job to care for a parent.
- If you are a woman, you have changed your routine as far as dress and makeup—changing to one that takes less time.
- Your vacations are spent caring for a parent.
- You feel tired and stressed and either get little sleep or want to sleep much of the day.
- You have relinquished some of the fun things you used to do and have not kept up with friendships and family gatherings.
- Your spouse or children have complained about your lack of attention to them.
- You are beginning to resent the parent you are helping to care for.

Taking on the responsibility of your elderly parent's care can consume your time if you let it. And if you are dealing with a parent who has a debilitating medical condition such as a stroke, you may find that you have suddenly lost control of your life. The caregiver's role is just suddenly thrust upon you and you do not have much choice in the matter.

Become an Advocate

As a caregiver, you become an advocate for your elderly parents. Those who know how to work the system, who will admit to themselves, "I can't do it all by myself," and those who say in a firm voice, "I need to take care of myself, too," will survive and grow from the experience. The person being cared for will also benefit from the caregiver's desire to remain a total person, unbroken by the demands of a role that too often becomes the focus of their lives.

Time and again, whether from family members or professional medical gerontologists, I've heard the phrase, "It helps if you know how to use the system." But before we can use this "system," we have to know what it is and how it works. I discuss this further in the chapters "Where to Get Help" and "Who Pays?".

The elderly population is growing by leaps and bounds, propelling the relatively new field of gerontology into rapid growth. But there is not yet a uniform social service system for the aging. It is still in its infancy. The help and services available are not clearly defined. What works in one part of the country, state or county may not yet be established in another. Sometimes a visiting nurse may offer insights into where to get assistance. Many times it will be another caregiver who has learned first hand where to turn for support in a particular situation. It's been stated that we need what is called "a point of entry" into the system. Sometimes we have to grope just to find where such a point might exist.

Once you gain access to the system, the next step as an advocate is to get appropriate help for your parent. I learned this the hard way with my mother's care. I spoke earlier of how, soon after my mother was diagnosed with Alzheimer's, she became inactive and sat around staring with a glazed look in her eyes. Part of this was the result of her knowing of her diagnosis. She was plainly depressed. Alzheimer's had already been a part of her life. Three of her eight brothers and sisters had the symptoms of the disease before their deaths. So had her mother. Another contributing factor to her depression turned out to be a medication she was given called Dilantin. This drug promotes sodium loss from nerve fibers, which in turns lessens excitability and inhibits the spread of nerve impulses. In other words, it was deadening her.

Within a short period of time, the physician who had administered that medication retired and a new doctor took her case. He immediately took her off Dilantin and placed her on vitamin B-12. Her mood improved within weeks. Had I, or other members of my family, been aware of the debilitating effects of the drug prescribed to her, we could have questioned its use early on. But that experience taught us all a lesson. We have the right to question the treatment given our loved ones. We have, indeed, an obligation to keep track of all phases of their care.

At the same time, we have to take care of ourselves if we are going to effectively care for our parents, and survive the experience intact. For me, an important part of surviving has been my positive outlook. For the past several years, while I have been slowly accepting my grief over my mother, who for all intents and purposes is not the mother I have known in the past, I have at the same time been enjoying and loving her. During that time, she has been able to enjoy the company of her grandchildren and great-grandchildren, and use her sense of humor at the most outrageous times.

Yes, I wear rose-colored glasses, which I've always thought is rather healthy. So do some health professionals who are finding out that people who are realistic, but who look on the bright side of things, seem to fare better than the Chicken Littles of society who see the sky falling at every turn. This positive attitude got me through my mother's mastectomy after cancer was discovered last year, and through my dad's back surgery which eventually sent him into depression.

Helping my parents through that rough period in their lives wasn't a matter of sitting back and letting life take its course. My sister and I consulted with the oncologist who was to perform the mastectomy. We made ourselves aware of alternatives and exactly what the situation portended. We consulted with my father, and made the decisions together. After my father's back surgery, when he didn't respond as he should have, we contacted the physicians and let them know we wanted something done. We contacted service agencies and my parents' minister to get a list of people my father could call on for help when it was needed in a pinch, and we let him know we were there to help when needed, but not to take over or interfere.

This soft type of advocacy, in which we didn't force our parents to accept help but made ourselves available when needed, paid off in the long run. When the bad times really hit after my dad's stroke, being knowledgeable, forewarned and enlightened eased the stress of the situation by enabling us to effectively help our parents and by giving us some measure of control. This is not to say that there haven't been days since that have proven worse than anything I ever anticipated, such as when we began trying to get our parents into the **Medi-Cal*** system.

Studies by K. Kiemele, J. Garrard and K. Feldt of the University of Minnesota, show that caregivers of Alzheimer's patients who participated in programs that provided information about the disease process, legal/financial concerns, daily care techniques and who knew about caregiver relief issues, remained healthier than those who didn't have the information. My parents were raised at a time when physicians were thought of as gods, so they have never questioned them. My sister and I do, however. Neither did they question public agencies or authorities. We most certainly do.

Even armed with these attitudes, I was scared at that first flash of terror and the thought that my life was changing without my permission. That first call from Dad a year before his stroke, "I need help," threw me into a quandary. I had a book to complete on a deadline; animals to care for; two houses—one a rental—to tend; and it was a long drive to their home from my place. Visions of the worst flashed through my mind. How was I going to continue working if I was needed someplace else? My immediate reaction was panic. I was ready to make a convalescent case out of both of them, and a basket case out of me.

We're always going to be unprepared for that first call, but the problem can grow worse if we don't face it. What I learned from my own experience, is that if you

*Terms appearing in bold italics are defined in Chapter 8, "Who Pays."

spend the time to research and find appropriate help, the job can get done without making a shambles of your life. You become an advocate, not a martyr. I try to keep that in mind as conditions change and I go farther into the black hole.

The Martyr's Role

I know better than to get myself into the role of martyr. The halo wouldn't fit anyway. The facts are that about thirty-one percent of caregivers are in the work force, and twenty percent of them have children under eighteen years old. Everyone who is a caregiver has other obligations. Some caregivers are ill themselves.

I looked on my father as a hero for caring for my mother like he did. My sister and I were worried at the onset of my mother's diagnosis of Alzheimer's that he wouldn't be up to caring for her. He's always sort of had the attitude that, "Well, if I don't worry about it, it will go away." But he managed quite well with the responsibility, in part because he was able to laugh at life's inconsistencies. Unfortunately, the fact that my father took full responsibility for my mother's care may have led to his stroke. Whether I like the idea or not, I know that full-time family-member caregivers suffer an inordinate amount of stress and their duties often lead to their own deaths.

My father had hidden the fact that Mom refused to bathe, needed constant supervision or she would wander off, was slightly incontinent, had to be reminded to eat, and required a host of other minor necessities that kept

Dad busy from morning to night. He could get away with this deception, partly because my mother, like many Alzheimer's patients, often appeared quite normal in social situations. Unfortunately, family and friends seldom see the daily reality of the caregiver's role. When a caregiver complains, others are often unsympathetic because they don't understand. Most of my parents' neighbors and friends had no idea my mother was in such bad shape until after Dad's stroke, and after she attempted suicide and was placed in a psychiatric ward.

On the other hand, although my father refused to get outside help ("Mama wouldn't like that," he'd say), he felt that caring for her was his responsibility and he did it out of love and affection. In many ways, I admire how my father cared for my mother even though it may have shortened his life. When we look at others who are caring for their loved ones, it should be with nonjudgmental eyes. We simply don't know the degree of their suffering.

We also need to look within ourselves with these same nonjudgmental perspectives. Most of us will do the best we can. If we start believing we're the "only" ones who can do the job and are capable of such self-sacrifice, and that we are solely responsible for the care of our loved ones, we set ourselves up for a fall. If we do this, we need to question our own motives.

We read or hear about a caregiver shooting a spouse after a marriage of fifty or more years. Or a couple who commit suicide together following a long and happy marriage. We shouldn't be so shocked. Severe stress can, and does, lead to such tragedies. My shock was at how my father was able to care for my mother as long as he did.

Not Everyone Can Give Care

I have a friend who acknowledges that, "I literally ran from my mother when it came time that she needed help. She tried for years to get me to let her move in with my family and I dodged it every chance I got. Thank heavens I had a sister-in-law who took her in." This woman and her mother had never gotten along. Her memories are of a mother who derided her constantly as a child, whose hateful venom sent her into therapy as an adult, whose abuses, though not leaving her scarred physically, left her mentally distraught.

Several years have passed since her mother's death, and she now understands some of the problems that drove her mother to fits and tirades. Until these issues were solved, however, it would have been disastrous for this woman, her own family and her mother to have become involved in a charade that might have injured all of them.

At some point in our lives, we have to make peace with our parents and in some cases, this may not be possible. The best we can do is make peace with ourselves concerning our parents. A psychiatrist friend of mine said, "Usually, a person rebels against their parents in their teens and this is the healthiest and most normal time to do it. If they wait until they are in their twenties, it's going to be harder and more vitriolic. If they're in their thirties, it's going to be even more difficult, but not impossible. If they're in their forties before they try to make peace with them, they usually end up in therapy."

Entering a caregiving situation begins with unconditional love, and if that is lacking, it will be a burdensome experience.

❤   ❤   ❤

Nancy T., a victim of child abuse, says she can never make this peace with her parents. She moved to Chicago from her hometown in California with her husband several years ago (he's now deceased) and returns to California for periodic visits. But she says that's as close as she's getting, even though her parents are aged and need some care. She was molested by her stepfather as a child—a fact her mother has never acknowledged.

Try as she might, and with good reason, she will never take care of them. On her visits, she has helped them get their business in order, made suggestions on how to better deal with their infirmities, but she refuses to move back near them even though she'd like to move back to California. She is simply too uncomfortable around them for any extended period of time.

There are other extenuating circumstances to prevent caregiving. The person to be cared for may live in another state. Perhaps the potential caregiver is in bad health, or already caring for a handicapped child. Maybe they are suffering a trauma of their own. But for those of us who choose to provide care and believe we come from the happiest of families, it is crucial to settle any unresolved feelings we have about our parents before we can deal effectively with the new role we've been thrust into.

Who Gives Care

At some point in our lives, many of us, especially if we are women, will care for an aging parent. We may not have total responsibility for that care, but, on average, we will spend approximately eighteen years assisting an elderly parent. Thirty-three percent of all caregivers are the sole providers of that care.

Stories are rife about older members of our society being thrust into nursing homes by uncaring relatives when, in fact, only about five percent of those over sixty-five are institutionalized, and ten percent of those eighty-five or older. The majority who need care get help from family members. Adult children usually assist in caregiving duties or have the full responsibility at some point in their lives, even when the parent is institutionalized. It is a giant myth that the elderly are "dumped" by their children in this society. There are cases where an elderly person is alone and forgotten, but it is more rare than usual.

Approximately seventy to eighty percent of caregivers are women. Women are often considered expert nurturers, and many come from a lifetime of giving to others. But this background can diminish their objectivity. Women also experience difficulty being taken seriously by doctors and administrators. A Rush University study, reported at the 1989 Gerontological

Society meeting, stated that traits typically associated with masculinity, such as power and management skills, are crucial to the success of caregivers.

Minority women are more likely to be caregivers and are more likely to be forced to balance the demands of caregiving and paid employment. Fifty percent of all caregivers are also working outside the home, most of them full time. Of those who work, many end up taking time off, quitting their jobs, or taking early retirement in order to keep up with their caregiving duties. One-third of family caregivers live in poverty.

The average age of the caregiver is fifty-seven, with twenty-five percent of them between ages sixty and seventy-five. Ten percent of those caring for the aged are more than seventy-five years old.

Statistics, however, don't touch on the human problems of caregiving in the twentieth century, and researchers are just beginning to forecast the caregiving picture for the twenty-first century. Home care will be a necessity. There simply won't be the funds for institutional care, nor the number of nursing homes necessary.

Getting Help

It's important for caregivers to reach out for support. The help is available and growing. Some agencies now provide hot lines to call for help; others have services that put caregivers who are unable to leave the home in touch with other caregivers by telephone for mutual support. Some areas provide day care for the elderly that enables the caregiver to get away for awhile. And there are other support sources for caregivers.

Some states are looking at family leave for workers who need to take time off from work to help family members. Twenty-eight states have introduced legislation for family leave in the workplace, although only four (Connecticut, Rhode Island, Oregon and Minnesota) have enacted such laws. Two bills pending in Congress would require companies to offer unpaid leaves of absence for employees assisting elderly dependents. But the majority of companies oppose such laws.

Yet, some companies are starting to offer elder-care provisions such as assistance in finding care for elderly parents and relatives; leaves of absence for elderly care patterned after maternity leave; counseling and referral services; on-site elder care; and programs for setting aside pre-tax earnings for elder care.

Another innovative program is a statewide, private, nonprofit, licensed care management agency, sponsored by Connecticut Community Care, Inc., that offers choices to families caring for a disabled person. Begun in the 1970s as a funded program, it is now self-sufficient and serves as a model for other states trying to find solutions to long-term care. Its goal is to keep the elderly person independent as long as possible by providing services in the home to them. Another of their services is to offer counseling to employers about how to retain their caregiving employees. Counseling is also available for the employee.

All of these trends, from government-backed programs to those introduced by the marketplace, will aid the elderly and those who are charged with their care. But until these programs become commonly available, caregivers will have to seek them out. The time spent in the search is worth the trouble.

The Growing Number of Elderly

The number of Americans sixty-five years or older increased to 25.5 million in 1980, accounting for 11.3 percent of the population, up from 9.9 percent in 1970, according to the 1980 census. This trend is expected to continue, and the numbers of elderly may reach seventeen percent of the population near the turn of the century and twenty-two percent by the year 2030.

If only we could all have the stamina of George Burns, who's scheduled to play London's Palladium Theatre on his one hundredth birthday, aging would be a more positive, uplifting experience. But the reality is that the majority of elderly don't make it to old age without health problems. However, our definitions of old age are changing. On the whole, our older population is better educated, healthier and more active than previous generations.

These trends are not only taking place in the United States. Worldwide, the number of elderly is increasing 2.4 percent annually, faster than the growth in the global population as a whole, which is at 1.7 percent annually. This growth in the numbers of elderly means power.

As witnessed by groups such as the Gray Panthers, our older citizens aren't going to sit back and be forgotten. They're out there fighting for their rights, long neglected in a nation that has worshipped the young.

Along with these rights will come a more realistic look at caregivers. Unfortunately, few government programs and social services support home care. Additionally, those studying what has been termed, "The graying of America," say that in the future, there simply won't be enough money or institutions to handle the growing numbers of the aged. Thus, incentives will be given to make it attractive to keep the elderly at home for as long as possible.

The truth is, most of us want to care for our elderly parents when possible. What we don't want to do is diminish their dignity or ruin our emotional or physical health in the meantime. Nor is this what most of the elderly want. They want to remain independent, stay in their own familiar surroundings and retain their own identities.

Changes in the Family Structure

We once counted on Mama, but now my sister and I, and other members of the family, have taken over. My children have asked if they can come to my house for Thanksgiving. They also asked if they could bring most of the Thanksgiving dinner this year, in an effort to relieve me of some of the work while I stumbled through the first phase of getting the necessary help for my parents and tending to their business. In a sense, my own children have become caregivers because they are looking out for my interests and quality of life.

My life, and those of other family members, will never be the same again, but that would have been true whether or not my mother acquired Alzheimer's or Daddy had a stroke. Life is in constant change and it's impossible to go back and recapture my mother as someone I can lean on.

Psychologist Angela Rosenberg of the College of St. Scholastica in Minnesota says that middle-aged daughters aren't happy "mothering" their aging mothers. Her studies show that adult daughters prefer a relationship of more equal give-and-take and consider their mothers an important source of support. But as their mothers age, that becomes less likely. "The potential for stress is clear," says Rosenberg. "Daughters are losing their mothers' support at the same time they are shouldering the additional strain of caregiving."

Mother-daughter relationships appear to be more intimate than father-daughter, or even father-son, relationships, she says. We tend to continually look to our mothers as nurturers and to lose that nurturing is distressing.

She points out that the emotions involved in this phase of a mother-daughter relationship haven't been addressed much by mental health professionals. Daughters who are having problems handling the changing relationship with their mothers should talk with other women, form support groups, seek counseling when necessary, or talk with the mother about it if they have the kind of relationship in which they can confront one another openly.

Added to this confusion in changing roles between mother and daughter are the natural age changes occurring to the caregiver. There are exceptions, but usually we step into the role of caregiver at a time when we're reevaluating our own lives. Often our children have recently left home, or have been gone a few years, bringing about a natural transition in our lives. According to psychologist David S. Holmes of the University of Kansas, the effects on women at this time are characterized by a personal mellowing and improved marital relations.

This particular transition has followed on the heels of our greatest marital dissatisfaction, personal disruption and decreased personal development. Most of our energy, until now, has been focused on our children. So when we enter this next phase, we're making peace with our married life, starting to reach out again toward personal development and settling in—taking a new look at ourselves, and perhaps, setting new goals. We become more aware of the aging process and develop a sense of the finiteness of life, Holmes says.

In many instances, women between the ages of fifty-five and sixty reported to Holmes that the growth in their personal lives was hindered somewhat by responsibilities associated with the care of aging parents and relatives. "This doesn't affect men as greatly as women because caregiving usually falls to the women. Men get it second hand by how the wives are feeling.

Men are usually affected more by this when they are responsible for caring for a wife and no one else is there," he says.

On the whole, men aren't as affected by a mid-life crisis as much as women despite earlier reports to the contrary, Holmes says. "They have some of the symptoms, but not to the degree women do. In other words, not all men run off with some eighteen-year-old tootsie."

Regardless of how dramatic or minor these changes may be for men and women at mid-life, it is a recognized transition period and like any change it's fraught with danger signals that need recognition and action. Taking on the care of a parent at this time can add to the strain of change. "It's very important for the couple to attend support groups. This helps because they see that others are going through the same thing caring for parents with chronic illness. They share information. Mostly though, they just have to get through it," he says.

Profiles of Caregivers 2

OUR BACKGROUNDS, ASSORTED FAMILY STYLES, different faiths, personal health issues, outlook on life, financial status, inherited personalities—all play a part in the choices we make concerning caregiving. What works for one person may not prove viable for another. But we all have a lot to learn from the trials and errors of other caregivers who have faced similar circumstances to our own. They can help us know what to expect in getting appropriate care for our parents. The following are some of their stories.

A Job Well Done

The day after his mother's funeral, Leslie Johnson (not his real name) received a call from a good friend who said, "Congratulations. You did it your way. You did the best you could with your dad and mom and now your job is finished." Les acknowledged he was at first stunned by what his friend had to say. He recalled that most people had been using words like "sorry" and "grief" when talking to him. Later, he realized his friend's words were the kindliest, most helpful sentiments anyone could have expressed.

The decision he had made nearly six years before to help care for his parents had affected every aspect of his life. As the oldest son, he'd been required to make decisions that alienated siblings, angered his mother, and placed unanticipated burdens on his own family, finances and sometimes his friends. But if he had to do it all over again, the only thing he would change is his decision not to tell his father that he (his father) was dying of cancer.

His main source of support during those years was his wife, Nancy, who helped shoulder the care of first his father and then his mother, while raising her own family, and holding down a full-time job.

They began their role as caregivers knowing nothing of the system. The areas they ventured into were new to them and they had no one to guide them. What they did have was a strong feeling of commitment and for them, it worked, although not always smoothly. They took on the responsibility of providing care for their parents and they sought help from whatever sources they could tap.

This couple's story, like many others, echoes the underlying theme that most people don't relish the idea of being caretakers of family members. It's just something that comes to us in the normal processes of life. "This sort of thing sometimes just falls on the oldest son. It's usually the strongest one of the family who steps forward. Or he or she simply doesn't step backwards fast enough," Les says.

Les's father was diagnosed with inoperable cancer little more than five years ago. At the time, his mother was in a convalescent hospital recuperating from a broken hip. "My dad was having trouble breathing and I took him to the hospital. The doctors told me that he had inoperable cancer and wouldn't live longer than six months."

When Les's mother heard that her husband, Leslie Sr., was sick, she took a turn for the worse. But the family convinced her that she needed to get well so that she could help take care of him. She wasn't told that he only had six months to live. She got well enough to go home after a three-month stay at Les's home. With the help of a housekeeper and Nancy and Les, his father and mother were able to get by in their own home.

Les recalls helping Leslie Sr. shave and take a shower, and realizing that it was difficult for this proud and self-assured man to accept his help. "When we were through, I'd ask him, 'Do you feel better now, Pop?' and he'd say, 'Yeah, well, this is OK.' I was afraid he'd be resentful. But I think he understood and appreciated it. But he had that look in his eye. He knew he was dying."

Les and his wife had already made the decision to help care for him at home for as long as possible. That decision was made after doctors told Les that by law, they would have to hook Leslie Sr. up to life-support systems if he stayed in the hospital. This would lengthen his life, but in the end make it unbearable because of the pain. Hospital staff had trained Les to give his father morphine when necessary.

The doctor suggested that Les and Nancy take a vacation before the final bout with the cancer began. They were in Mexico when word reached them that Leslie Sr. had died of a heart attack. "Dad was fortunate that he died like that," Les says.

Following his death, however, Les's mother decided that she no longer wanted to live. "She felt she had no reason to live. She suffered what was believed to be a stroke, but after about ten days, the doctor said everything was OK and we took her to our house. But she got progressively worse. The quality of her life was garbage, mainly because of her attitude.

"We tried as hard as we could. We had a therapist come in but she wouldn't do the exercises they taught her. Finally the therapist said, 'There's no sense in my coming back.' Mom just laid there and got to a point where she couldn't get better. One day in bed and you lose fifteen percent of your strength. It's a miracle that she could get up and go to the bathroom."

The choice was made, mostly by Les, that they would get a full-time housekeeper to help provide care at his mother's home, which was what she wanted. Les and his two brothers and their wives took turns on weekends caring for her so the housekeeper could have time off.

"It would have been better if Mom had stayed with us at our house rather than us running back and forth to hers," Les says. "I would have tried to get her up out of bed more—forced her to—and she would have done better. The quality of her life would have improved."

During the week, Nancy did the shopping, transported her mother-in-law to the doctors and did other errands as the need arose. She and Les also brought Les's mom to all the family functions and celebrations she agreed to attend. "I had some reservations about asking Nancy to help, but she wanted to do it and it's hard for me to understand that. How can you feel so responsible when it's not even your own parents? At first, I felt like I couldn't lay that responsibility on Nancy.

"My brothers and their wives didn't want to help at first. But when we took her home, I simply laid out a schedule for everyone. I felt it was my responsibility to do that. I tried to make it regimented so we could at least plan our lives. I didn't ask them. I told them: 'This is what we're going to do.' If I had asked, they would have gotten out of it." The plan Les devised worked pretty well for him and his family, although it got to be too much for one of his brothers after about a year and he offered to pay for help on the weekend when it would have been his turn.

"If you don't do the things you think you should do to help, you feel guilty. A lot of this whole operation was out of guilt." But Les sees nothing wrong with a little bit of guilt if it will motivate people to make choices they won't regret later. "When all is said and done, you should do it for your own good. I can go on with my life and won't have to say, 'I wish I had done so-and-so.' You just do those things you should do. Some moralists and philosophers say we're not responsible, but I still feel responsible.

"I tried to make it as easy on everyone as I could, including myself. I told Mom she wasn't going to a convalescent home. I could have washed my hands of her, but I would have felt like a jerk the rest of my life. Even though it wasn't the best care—not professional—it was better than an institution. We did the best we could."

A few months prior to her death, Les's mother became incontinent and he started thinking about putting her in a convalescent home. He contacted the administrator of one in Culver City, California, with an excellent reputation, and put her on the waiting list. But when the time came, he decided to wait a little longer. His mother seemed to be getting better, and her incontinence was under control. This on-again, off-again decision went on for months and he never did come to a firm decision. It remained something he was "just about to do."

Les's major concern was how his wife was holding up under the strain since she was helping so much. "I didn't want Mom to go into a home, but I would have made that decision over Nancy's protest if I had had to. There are things you just have to do. Despite my concern for my mother and father, my wife comes first and if I had seen that it was too much, I would have stopped it." Les acknowledges that there were many times when he just wanted to chuck the whole thing. "She didn't want to live and it made it unbearable for everyone else. Sometimes I got discouraged about the whole thing."

In addition to the responsibilities of providing care, Les and Nancy also worked through a maze of legalities to get the needed care, and the means to pay for it. At the onset, his parents were pretty secure. They owned their home, although they had a small loan against it for some remodeling. Both drew Social Security and his father had a retirement income from his former place of work. They were able to pay for a housekeeper during the day.

But when his father died, his mother lost the retirement income and the additional social security check. She was living on about $600 per month. Since she needed full-time care, Les and Nancy contacted a nonprofit resource center in Santa Monica, California, connected with the Catholic Church that had provided the housekeeper used by the senior Johnsons in their home before the father's death. The center was a gathering place for Mexican-Americans, most who couldn't speak English, but who needed jobs.

A visiting nurse who came to check on his mother, told them they were probably eligible for some help with in-home services through **Medi-Cal**, which gives medical financial assistance to low-income families. They obtained applications from the state **Medi-Cal** office and then it was determined exactly how many hours of care the state would pay for, based on his mother's needs.

Normally, the hired caretaker would be paid directly by the state, but since the caretaker they had chosen didn't have her citizenship papers, the check was mailed to Nancy who then deposited it in a special account they had set up for her mother-in-law. Aminda, the caretaker, who eventually obtained her citizenship with the help of the Johnsons, was paid from this fund. "We opened the special account so we would have a record of the distribution of money in order that other members of the family would know where it was being spent," Nancy said.

The Johnsons had to pay taxes on the caretaker's money sent to them in Nancy's name, and it was decided by the entire family that these tax payments would be reimbursed to Nancy and Les after their mother's death.

All of this was spelled out in a **living trust** that was established for his mother's estate. This particular type of trust protects an estate from probate and court expenses. It costs from $800 to $1,000 in attorney fees to establish, but Les says it was a bargain for his family in the long run.

"It might seem a cold thing to do," Les says, "and lots of families avoid it. They don't want to talk about death, and it is difficult to talk about it. You can't just walk up to your mom or dad and say, 'You're getting along. What are you going to do about this stuff?' The ideal situation is for the parents to have enough wherewithal to approach the children. I was kind of apprehensive when I first talked to my dad about writing a will, but he just said, 'I don't have much to leave you guys. I only have the house, but I want you guys to have it all.'

"I said, 'OK, Dad. I'll fix it up.' There are organizations that have lawyers who donate their time to seniors. For a minimum fee of $35 they will help you write a simple will, and that's what we did." His father died before he had time to sign the will, which didn't present too much of a problem since everything goes to the widow in California unless otherwise stipulated.

After his dad's death, Les was sort of "floundering around," when it came time to make arrangements for the funeral. None of his father's wishes had been put in writing. The funeral director was a big help. He asked Les questions about his father's background and sent him on some leads. The family could have been saved much grief if there had been a signed will stipulating the wishes of the deceased.

As it turned out, Les's father was eligible for government funds of $150 toward the funeral and burial in a nearby military cemetery since he was a World War I veteran. This service did not jump at Les out of thin air. He had to call one agency after another, sometimes being passed from one spokesperson to another. The only hitch to it was that his father would have to be cremated because of lack of space at the cemetery. Les didn't know how his mother or the rest of the family would react to that. They were, however, in agreement. He also found out that his mother, upon her death, would be eligible to be buried with his father.

When the ordeal with his father was over, they started over again with his mother. Les grappled with the problem of how to approach his mother. "I told her she should make the legal and financial matters easier for us.

I think you have to do that the best way you know how. It makes you feel cruel, mean and money-grubbing. But if you don't do it, the house will have to sit in probate for two years and then the state will take forty to sixty percent of everything."

When Les broached the subject of a **living trust**, his mother accused him of trying to take everything away from her. "I told her I wasn't coming over anymore and I stayed away two weeks until she apologized." Les worried that other family members might accuse him of taking everything away as well. "I wondered if other family members were thinking I would try to move in and take things. But I couldn't let that bother me."

Now that it's all over, Les and Nancy can get back to a more normal routine in life. They're glad they took on the role of caregivers and say it taught them many things.

Although they're only in their early fifties, they've anticipated a time when they might not be capable of taking care of themselves, and have discussed it and prepared for it with their grown children. They've established a **living trust** in the names of their children and they talk about death with them. They don't want their children to have to play the "bad guys" like they did.

"Caregiving is tough in any family" Les says. "You've made your own little niche and then this comes along and messes it up. But it's just the right thing to do."

Giving Too Much

Phyllis A. (not her real name), who lives in a Southern California beach community, is unhappy with her lifetime role as a caregiver, but is beginning to understand the circumstances that led to her entrapment. She had an unhappy childhood perpetrated by an extremely domineering mother and father. She's finally finding peace and adventure after a lifetime of caring for others.

She's exploring the possibilities of what she can do with the rest of her life since retiring as a manager at a major corporation. It took professional therapy for her to unravel the circumstances and personality traits that led to her lifetime of caregiving. She acknowledges she still has a long way to go before she's free of the need to devote her life to others by giving up her own.

It's a trap many of us are capable of falling into as we step into the role of caring for loved ones. Often we don't recognize what we've become and resent someone telling us that we need to get on with our own lives. We don't believe that anyone can help us because they wouldn't do as good or caring a job as we are doing.

"I've been a caretaker all my life," says Phyllis. "Mom took care of my grandmother when I was little and eventually I shared those duties with her. Grandma was a crabby old woman who had arthritis and I didn't much like her, but I didn't recognize or admit to those feelings as a child. I grew up Catholic and those weren't Christian feelings." She had lots of negative feelings during those early years and she confided them to a priest who didn't relieve her feelings of guilt. "I'm a lapsed Catholic now, but the feelings of guilt never go away."

Her family was also Italian and placed emphasis on the family sticking together. Phyllis was twenty-five and still living at home when her grandmother died. She hadn't yet begun to date. "In those days, good girls didn't move out of the house unless they got married. So there I was at home, and then my mother got sick. I think it was the stress of caring for my grandmother that brought on my mother's heart attack. So I stayed to help care for her. She couldn't do any heavy work.

"When I was growing up, there weren't the options there are today. We were just here to take care of the families. In my neighborhood there were lots of grandmas living with their families."

Phyllis graduated from high school and went to work, but kept caring for her mother when she was home. "My mother, as sweet and warm as she was, let me know she couldn't make it without me. That registered in my data bank for all eternity. I see now that she even sabotaged things like my dieting. Maybe it was a way of ensuring that I'd never find anyone who would want to marry me. She'd encourage me at first and be very enthusiastic. But little by little, she'd start doing things like baking my favorite cookies and saying, 'Come on, one won't hurt you.' So, little by little, I gave in."

When her mother died in 1970, Phyllis at first thought, Oh boy. I'm free now. "I was forty-one and I still hadn't moved. But Dad was a basket case by the time of Mom's death, so I stayed around to care for him."

She went into therapy when she was fifty. Ironically, the therapist was a Catholic nun who encouraged her to move out of the house and make a life of her own. Even after moving out, though, she continued to run errands and clean the house for her father, who had emphysema. Just prior to her father's death, she started getting other help for him because she couldn't handle it all with her job. Her father died three years ago and again, she felt "free."

Now her brother, who is diabetic and who is being treated for depression, is seeking her help. "I take him to the doctor's, the therapist, to support groups...it's a never-ending cycle," she says. "I talked him into going to a retirement home and I felt guilty about it. He wasn't eating properly and I felt guilty about that."

"It's funny how you can love somebody, and I do love my brother, but you can look at them and hate some of the things they do. I play games with him trying to get him to take care of himself. I put off doing things for him until it gets critical and then I do them because he won't."

Phyllis has become aware through counseling that she puts herself in these predicaments. "It's a way that I can have control." This type of control is similar to the control exercised by co-dependents of alcoholics. The co-dependent plays all sorts of roles—martyr, abused person, caretaker, protector—all the while maintaining control because they look on this other person as "sick" and themselves as "healthy."

She's had a few relationships with men since her mother's death and acknowledges that the one she's now in involves a man who has problems. "Sometimes, I think my presence in his life is saving him, but other times I know if I ended the relationship, it wouldn't make any difference. Here I am a caretaker again and I could walk away from it. But I don't want to. I must be getting something out of it."

Phyllis believes that her story might help others who become caregivers. Yes, she believes children should help their parents and other family members, but that the motives for doing so need to be different than hers were. They should maintain a life of their own, seek outside help and not try to handle everything. "If I had it to do over I would still help, but I'd do it differently. I wouldn't give up my life to it."

The Ideal Situation

Linda and Bob Falconer, a couple in their late forties, believe they have the ideal situation for taking care of his mother in their home. They've built a large addition onto their house that allows everyone's privacy when needed, and a full-time housekeeper eases the strain for Linda who is home all day. They aren't wealthy but neither are they financially strapped and they have done careful planning to make it work.

Still, there are problems brought about by the change in their household. But they expected this and speak openly about it—to each other, to their children (one is still at home), to friends and to his mother.

"I don't think elderly people can live with their children until it becomes a necessity. If we had tried this five years ago, there would have been a lot of friction.

Now she's dependent, and it sounds terrible, but she'll cooperate because she needs help," Linda says. Bob agrees. "There's a lot of truth to that. As children we don't want to cross our parent's paths. It's a very uncomfortable situation. It's tough to have two people under the same roof who have both always been in charge. It's an adjustment."

They say the adjustment was, perhaps, easier for them than for others because they have close ties with their mothers. Both were raised solely by them without fathers in the home. "They were both mother and father, so we have lots of respect for them and we understand where they're coming from," Bob says. "We had good relationships with them when we were growing up."

Linda's mother, in her seventies, lives nearby and visits them frequently, often accompanying them on the many camping trips they take.

Bob's mother is ninety-one and was living alone and driving until she was eighty-five. His mother had also lived nearby until a few years ago when she moved into a retirement community. "She thought she would be happy there, but it wasn't what she thought it would be. She had expected the weather to be warmer than it was, and she thought she would make friends with others her own age. Funny thing is, those people don't go out very much. They stay pretty much to themselves."

They found out that most people in that community are couples and they don't want to help much because they're afraid of being around someone sick. "Older people don't want to help each other. They don't want the responsibility of taking care of someone else. They have enough trouble taking care of themselves," says Bob.

After several falls, Bob's mother was put into a nursing home for nine months until the remodeling at Bob's home was completed. "She rebelled against the nursing home. While the care was good, everybody was put in the hall at the same time in the morning. Everyone got up at the same time. There is a limited number of people there to help, so you may get help an hour after you need it. It's handling people as a commodity. It's not meanness. We were adjusting to the nursing home, but I saw a change in Mom. She became more dependent," recalls Bob.

Despite this dislike of the nursing home, Bob's mother has insisted a few times when she couldn't have her way that she wanted to go back. "There's no way she really wanted to go back," says Bob. "I told her not to say it anymore, and she's never mentioned it again. She knows it isn't a threat to me because I'll take her back. She's no different than anyone else. She'll find a way to use guilt. We all manipulate others like that.

"She's planning all these things she wants to do. She has big plans and I think that's wonderful. Well, even if it is ridiculous, I let her say it. I don't want to take her hopes away. You don't have to be practical. It's OK to deceive yourself. It might be healthy."

Linda recalls the difficulty of keeping his mother in their home for six weeks before the remodeling. She'd had a pacemaker put in and needed twenty-four-hour care. "I can sympathize with people who have no resources. I developed a lot of resentment because no one else in her family would help. Before we got the housekeeper, I couldn't go anywhere."

They've also had to adjust to Bob's mother's housekeeper/companion. "She's quite wonderful, but impossible at the same time," Linda says. Even with help and the right conditions, caring for someone consumes your life. "I get up thinking about it and go to bed with it on my mind. I've become a single subject person. That's all I can talk about," Linda says. However, because they're fairly new at caretaking, she thinks this will pass as they all settle in. "I hope it isn't always going to be that way. I'm not suffering from it now, it's just very consuming. These are just humps in life that I have to get over."

Drawing the Line

Connie Courtney of Fort Worth, Texas, tried overseeing both her mother's and mother-in-law's care, while at the same time working as a school counselor. Her mother suffers from near blindness and had a stroke a few months ago. Her mother-in-law is in the first stages of Alzheimer's. Both were living in their own homes, and Connie was running back and forth, trying to attend to their needs. Just prior to retirement, Connie spent two weeks in the hospital with a kidney infection and pneumonia. "It was plain neglect. I reached the point where I couldn't take care of them in their own homes anymore. So it was a little warning," she says.

No sooner had Connie retired when both her mother and mother-in-law started needing full-time care. Her mother broke her hip and her mother-in-law nearly burned herself to death in an accidental fire. It was clearly time to change tactics.

The two elderly women have been best friends most of their lives, and Connie enjoys good relationships with both of them. "I've already said my good-byes to them because they're not the same people I used to know. My own mother is very childish now."

During the time Connie took care of them in their own homes, her mother-in-law, Bebee, had continued to work as a nurse although she was in the early stages of Alzheimer's. Alzheimer's patients can function quite well following familiar routines, but as they get further into the disease, this becomes impossible, so Connie tried to watch for signs that it was time to change Bebee's care. Connie wanted to see that her mother-in-law was able to live a full life in her own home as long as possible. "But I almost waited too long," she recalls. When Bebee accidentally set the house afire and was badly burned, Connie decided that it was time to put her in a retirement home.

Now, Connie has to deal with a different set of problems. She feels guilty about putting Bebee in a home and Bebee exacerbates the situation by complaining about it. "I just spent an hour with my mother-in-law begging me to take her home from that place," Connie says. "But I can't do it." Connie describes the care her mother-in-law is getting as "minimal" at this point. And yet, she admits, "My mother-in-law is very social. That aspect of her brain is very alive and well. So, she does have a wonderful time at the facility. Sometimes, I beat up on myself for putting her in an institution. But then I ask myself, 'Why am I even thinking this?'"

Bebee had planned for her old age and has a health insurance policy, but it contains many contingencies. For example, if Bebee has to be moved from the retirement home to a nursing facility, she would first have to be hospitalized in order to still be covered by her policy. Connie and Bebee's physician make certain they comply with the regulations stated by the policy so that it will stay in effect.

Connie believes it's important for the caregiver to get to know the physician. "If I didn't have good rapport with her physician, I don't know what I would do. He reassures me that I've done the right thing by placing her in a home."

In between overseeing her mother-in-law's affairs and spending time with her, Connie also takes care of her own mother at home. Her husband, who owns his own construction firm, is gone much of the time and most of the responsibility is Connie's. Connie says she isn't bitter about shouldering most of the responsibility and simply accepts the reality of the situation. She knows it will end someday.

She has put all of her other plans on the back burner. She had planned on doing something with her art degree upon retirement. She had also planned to go back to school and get an advanced degree in counseling and establish her own practice. She fully believes these things will still happen, but she will feel better about herself if she does what she considers "the right thing" concerning her mother and mother-in-law. "Four years ago at Christmas I said, 'Let's all have a good Christmas because this might be our last all together.' Well, we keep making it for another Christmas."

Some of Connie's support comes from a close friend who is also caring for an aging parent. They spend time on the telephone together. "I don't have time to attend a support group," Connie says. "My day boils down to the TV going all day for my mother, while I make three meals and dash out to visit my mother-in-law." When friends come to visit, they bring sack lunches, "because they know I don't have the time to fix lunch for them."

Connie is in the process of clearing out the homes of her mother and mother-in-law—getting rid of and storing a lifetime of accumulations for the two women.

"I think the worst of it is behind me," says Connie. "My hope is that I've been able to maintain a healthy body. When the red flag goes up, I hope I pay attention to it. I know that I tend to get caught up in this. When I have errands, such as to the store or the library, I take my mother with me and she waits in the car. So far it works out OK. I hope I'll know the point when it's time for me to hire someone and get some help.

"Both of these women have had outstanding lives and I hope I can look back over it all and say that I gave them the best in their last years because it would be a shame to have it any different. I think that's important."

Becoming the Bad Guy

"There has to be what I call the 'bad guy' in the family. The one who makes the decision and gets the blame when things go wrong. You don't get the credit when things go right—no pat on the back—but it doesn't bother me anymore," says Marge N. (not her real name) of Virginia.

Marge and her husband made the difficult decision to place her mother in a nursing home. Friends have asked Marge, "How could you put your mother in a nursing home?" or "How could you spend your inheritance that way?"

To the first question Marge says, "You develop a sort of toughness. I know lots of people who are taking care of their parents in the home and are about to lose their minds. But they would have a guilt breakdown if they tried to change anything." As to the inheritance, she wants her mother to have the best care possible and if that care eats up the estate, so be it.

It isn't as if Marge has deserted her mother. Quite the contrary. She sees her everyday in the nearby nursing facility, tends to all of her business, oversees her care, and acts as an advocate for all her mother's affairs. The day I spoke with Marge on the phone, she was ironing her mother's clothes to take to her.

The advocacy began before her mother ever entered the nursing home, though. "Mom had started picking up her life after Dad died. He was seventy-seven and had been a diabetic for eighteen years. He had had three heart surgeries and a leg amputated. They kept going to Florida every year and she took good care of him. He was a good patient most of the time, but toward the end it was difficult. After he had his leg amputated, it became obvious that he needed to go into a nursing home. He understood it at first but then he became rebellious. He decided it should be like the good old days when a family retainer would stay with you around the clock. Well, Mom ended up with a breakdown in the hospital, and we had to tell Daddy that he wasn't going to be able to go home from the nursing home. It was tough on Mom at first.

"A few years after he died, I began noticing changes in her. One time I went to visit and she was telling me about how her grandsons had been there the night before and were fixing hamburgers in the kitchen." Marge asked her what she was talking about, since the grandsons were away at college, and her mother sheepishly replied, "Oh, I guess I was just imagining it." Marge told the rest of the family about the incident, but they told her she was making too much of it. "But the next day, I decided to go check on her anyway," Marge says. "She told me a woman was looking in the window at her."

Marge contacted her mother's physician, talked to her husband and other family members, but couldn't get anyone interested in the situation. Finally she called a geriatric specialist at the local university hospital and he agreed to see her mother. "I told him my mother would kill me if I went behind her back and saw another doctor. I told him Mom looked at her own doctor as if he were a god."

But she did take her mother to see him the next day, and during the wait in the office, her mother collapsed and was admitted to the hospital emergency ward. A physician came out to talk to Marge and began with, "How could you have allowed your mother to take this much medication?" Marge had no idea what the physician was talking about, but later found out that her mother's own physician had prescribed tranquilizers for her mother nearly twenty-five years previously and had never changed the prescription despite later adding heart and blood pressure medication.

Marge's mother was in a coma for sixteen days at this time and the family was told to go ahead and make funeral arrangements. But her mother recovered and was moved to a nursing home. At the time of admittance, Marge was told her mother would have to be admitted by her original doctor of record, who was the physician who had over prescribed the medication.

She was assured that all the misunderstandings had been straightened out, but a few days after her mother was admitted, the head nurse called from the nursing home and insisted that Marge get another physician for her mother. When Marge told her she'd been told she couldn't do that, the nurse whispered, "Listen, I'm putting my job on the line. I'm telling you your mother is going to die if you don't get that prescription changed right away. That doctor has put her back on the same stuff and in the same amounts."

From that point on, Marge became an advocate. She fired the old doctor and directed her mother's care, selecting another physician from the university hospital. She also challenges routines and treatment at the nursing facility, which has frequently changed administrations.

It took her mother two years to recover from the medication enough to be able to feed and take minimal care of herself. "Basically, Mom gets excellent care. It hasn't been without its ups and downs. It hasn't always been quality, but I'm there nearly every day and I ask questions. They know I'm going to be there, and they know I participate in family council meetings (meetings between the staff, administration and the families) and that I'm very outspoken. They don't like my complaints to come out in family council, so they take care of the things I complain about." Marge says she's had the training to stand up to people because she's been a teacher, had her own business and is involved in politics.

"I try to remember that this is the real world and I don't expect things to be perfect at the facility. Mom can be very abrasive if she doesn't get her own way. If someone rubs her the wrong way, there is nothing you can say that will make her understand that person."

She's also aware that most of the nurse's aides have very little training and are underpaid, which makes for a large turnover. Nevertheless, she remembers a time when she brought her mother something after visiting hours. Marge went over about 9:00 P.M. and there was no security. "Anyone could have walked into the wards and harmed a patient." So she raised a ruckus about it.

"Actually, I'm very blessed. Mom is getting excellent care and I'm able to have a life of my own. At one time,

I told my doctor that I couldn't handle the comments some people made about me putting my mother in a nursing home and he said I should be ready with the standard answer of, "Well, hey, if you're willing to take care of her, I'll bring her over tomorrow."

It would be nice if all elderly could live independently until the end as Marge's father-in-law did. She tells the story of how he came home from a shopping trip with her mother-in-law a few years ago and simply dropped dead. "That's a wonderful way to go," she says. "But that doesn't happen to everyone." She watched her own father go in a lingering way, and now her mother is deteriorating slowly. Also, she is starting to look after her mother-in-law who recently gave up her home and moved into a small apartment nearby.

Marge relates her experiences with her mother to her own children. "I remind them not to let me ever put them on a guilt trip. I don't look forward to being put in a nursing home, but who knows?"

Respecting Mom's Independence

Paula Morris is the thirty-four-year-old mother of an eighteen-year-old son. She was single for ten years, during which she started her life over in California and struggled through a career. A little over a year ago she remarried.

The youngest of six children, Paula got a taste of caregiving for the elderly when her seventy-eight-year-old mother, Pauline, visited her in 1988. One week after her arrival, Pauline suffered a massive heart attack. Paula continued working full time as office administrator for a group of psychiatrists and visited her mother during lunch breaks and in the evening after work. Keeping extra busy helped maintain her sanity.

It was determined that her mother needed bypass surgery, but her mother refused for several weeks. "She'd had angina since she was about forty and had had two minor heart attacks, but nothing like this. She was finally convinced that she was dying." The surgery was a success, but two days later, she had to have surgery on the veins from the angiogram because they hadn't gone back together. She had blood swelling that was life-threatening.

When she finally left the hospital, Pauline was too weak to travel, so Paula's new mother-in-law stayed with her during the day while Paula worked. Mother and mother-in-law argued so vehemently that the mother-in-law left. Two of Paula's sisters visited during this time, and eventually, her new father-in-law and his girlfriend helped care for her mother. They also used the services of a home-health-care nurse that was paid for by **Medicare**.

"It was an hysterical and chaotic time. Morris and I had only been married five months when it all happened. When my sisters came out to visit, the first one babied her and the second one was telling my mother to shut up. At this point, Morris and I figure that if our marriage could withstand what we were going through then, we must have a pretty good marriage."

Even then, it wasn't over. Before long, her mother had to go back into the hospital for internal bleeding.

They discovered five stomach ulcers that required surgery, with her mother again refusing until the last minute. At that point, Paula held her mother's hand and nearly forced her to sign the papers allowing the surgery. She was in the hospital again for two weeks and then home to Paula's house.

Her mother had arrived the first week in May for her visit and ended up staying until August 8. "By that time, she was glad to get on the plane to go home and I was glad to see her go," Paula says.

It didn't end once her mother got home to Pennsylvania, however. There were still decisions on whether or not her mother would continue to live alone or with another member of the family. Some of the family wanted to baby her mother and Paula was afraid it would make a lifetime invalid out of her. "My mom's always been independent and I felt it wasn't good to baby her.

"Actually, It was hard for me to relinquish control," Paula says. "They were even talking about putting her in a convalescent home temporarily and I was afraid that once that happened she would be there permanently. After she got home, she fell to pieces and didn't do so well. It took her longer to recuperate because they were babying her so. Of course it caused me anxiety. It was like sending a newborn baby away. I had looked after her for months and then I no longer had jurisdiction."

Although her mother did recuperate, Paula believes that eventually she'll move in with one of her sisters back home. If not, Paula would, at this point in her life, take care of her mother rather than have her put in a convalescent home. Taking care of her might not have been an option a few years ago when she was single, but now she would be capable of doing it. She would ask help from her brothers and sisters for what **Medicare** wouldn't cover, and she would expect to help financially if one of the other family members took her in. "Of course, if I had a choice I wouldn't want to take care of my parents. But they didn't say no to me when I was a child.

"Mom is so independent. Out loud she says she doesn't want any of her children taking care of her, but down deep she's saying, 'You're my children and you better take care of me.'"

❤   ❤   ❤

Caring for our elderly parents forces us to face tough issues. An Hispanic friend of mine, Leah Hernandez, told me about an uncle of hers who had to change his father-in-law's diapers. She said he wore gloves "to save them both embarrassment. It seemed to put a distance between my uncle and his father-in-law. And it was good. We must remember that it was probably more difficult and humiliating for this aging, old man to lose control of his bowels, than it was for my uncle to change him."

When I've talked to my own children about the possibility of me contracting Alzheimer's, since it seems to run in the family on my mother's side, I can tell it is difficult for them to see me that way. The truth is, and I don't like to think about it, I may need help one day. My children may become caregivers.

I hope that more help becomes available for the caregivers of my children's generation; that the financial burden of elder care will be addressed in this country and not leave families destitute; and that working husbands and wives who are caring for elderly parents will be understood and accommodated in the workforce.

Some of the caregivers who have been interviewed for this book were just entering "empty nest periods" and were set to enjoy this special time of their lives. Many others are of the "sandwich generation"—they still have children at home. Studies show that more than half of those caring for a parent are also caring for children under seventeen—one-third have children under twelve.

Many of their lives are in turmoil. They're stressed, sometimes bewildered, working through upheavals in their lives and those of their loved ones, including spouses and children. But still they are caring for their elderly parents. Whatever their reasons are for providing this care, and there are many, the bottom line is they are all doing the best they can, often under circumstances that we wish could be made easier, better, more rewarding and more relaxed. These caregivers tell us, however, that despite setbacks, lack of help, poor resources, family turmoil and few government interventions, they are getting the job done anyway.

If more of us become advocates for elder care in this country, things will be made a little easier for these caregivers in the future.

And, although sometimes it may seem impossible to get through a difficult period, you are not alone. Many others have travelled along the path you're on. It is the dance of time that we are struggling with—keeping in step with the rhythms sometimes makes us stumble and fall. Most of us, however, get up again, especially if we prepare ourselves with knowledge and allow others to lend us a hand.

Where to Get Help 3

CARING FOR THE ELDERLY ISN'T THE SAME TODAY as it was at the turn of the century when the majority of people lived in small towns surrounded by extended families who shared the responsibility of their care. The very old were fewer in number, since life expectancy wasn't so great as it is today, and those who did survive into old age were usually the heartiest types, since many of the diseases and infirmities that afflict the elderly today were not treatable then. They enjoyed what we consider a luxury today. They lived out their lives in familiar surroundings, with long-time friends and family members close by. Their caregivers usually worked near or in the home and had family support, so the burden of care wasn't placed on one person. If the primary caregiver was having problems, he or she could turn to a relative for comfort.

Since we don't have those close networks today, there are gaps in what the public needs and what is available. Many families who care for an elderly person are difficult to reach and serve. Americans tend to be fiercely independent and try to do everything on their own. Many caregivers are reluctant to seek help even though they may be juggling many other responsibilities, such as caring for their own families, holding down jobs and dealing with their own aging processes. They wait until the situation reaches a crisis point before getting help. By that time, it is often too late to forestall placing the elderly person in a nursing facility. The caregiver is simply too worn out.

I'm reminded of a woman whose husband has dementia. He broke her arm once when he was "confused," as she calls it. She refuses to give up caring for him.

I also know a 94-year-old woman who is caring for her 104-year-old sister. They have never gotten along but the younger sister feels obligated to care for her older sister. The older sister whacks the younger one with a cane sometimes and the younger sister reciprocates by leaving her older sister, who can barely move, lying on the floor for hours at a time when she falls. She screams at her to get her lazy bones up from the floor.

A study by Rhonda Montgomery of Wayne State University and Edgar Borgatta of the University of Washington, shows that in addition to caregivers being independent and reluctant to get help, they often lack the time and emotional resources to attend support groups or to tap into support services.

Many people feel ashamed or ignorant when seeking outside help with the problems associated with caregiving. However, caregivers who get some form of support are able to take better care of themselves. They are more aware of their limitations—that they can't take full responsibility for the care of their parents. This is the first step toward protecting your own health and that of your loved one.

The next step is getting the help you need—not a small feat since there is little help available for long-term care. Agencies, both public and private, are well aware of the need for solutions to long-term care and for assistance to those providing it. And organizations such as the American Association of Retired Persons, the Older Women's League, and the Gray Panthers are mostly responsible for having raised public consciousness about this problem.

Now some politicians are trying to force the government to take a more realistic look at the problems of elder care, and the government is starting to listen because of the escalating cost of caring for the frail elderly and those with dementia. Additionally, many private organizations, such as the National Academy of Elder Law and the Health Insurance Association of America, are focusing on care for the elderly and those who are giving the care.

Unfortunately, many of the programs now in existence are frequently overlooked by caregivers. I've spoken with many people who, like myself when my own parents started needing help, are completely unaware of where to find the support, information, and hands-on services they need. Ironically, I didn't find out until nearly a year after Dad's back surgery and a year before he suffered the stroke that a local agency could have provided immediate help for him when Mom went into the hospital for her mastectomy. The spokesperson for this agency, which provides services such as counseling for caregivers of Alzheimer's patients and other brain-damaged individuals, acknowledged that they have problems getting the word out about the help available.

What we look for again and again is that "point of entry"—an agency or knowledgeable person who can direct us to the proper sources. Since that point of entry is practically nonexistent, in many situations, we simply have to follow the bureaucratic paper and phone call trail that's often littered with anger and tears before we get help. Needless hours, days and even months are spent in frustration searching for the type of help each individual family needs. This was dramatically pointed out to me when my father suffered his stroke. Luckily, my mother was able to call my sister in Los Angeles about eighty miles away and tell her that my father had collapsed on the bathroom floor and had lost control of his bladder. My sister called a neighbor who got my father to the hospital and was waiting there with Mom until we arrived. After my sister notified the neighbor, she called me. I too live about eighty miles away.

In a flurry on that first day, we pooled our ideas and began calling around to get someone to come stay with Mother. Our first source was their church, and we did get someone, but she only lasted one day because her own sister died suddenly and she had to leave. So Mom stayed with my sister for a few days.

We began making lists of things to check—such as their social security, vehicle license and bank account numbers (since we would be paying the bills), birth dates and records and any other papers or forms to use when providing information to the agencies we knew we would be dealing with.

Since our names were on my parent's checking account, we immediately transferred nearly all the money into a special account in my sister's name so that she could pay bills and do the bookkeeping. In the ensuing weeks, as the bills came in, we found that my father had at least eleven charge accounts, with charges totaling more than $23,000—about $20,000 more than they had in their account. Acquainting yourself with your parent's financial business may seem an invasion of their personal lives, but it's a job you'll eventually have to do.

We knew early on that care for my parents wouldn't be covered by **Medicare*** for very long and that they didn't have the financial resources to pay for it themselves. Fortunately, we didn't have to "spend them down" to poverty level, so that they would be eligible for **Medi-Cal**. They were already more than eligible.

On day four of Daddy's hospital stay, we were told that he was going to be sent home. Since we hadn't found someone to care for Mom, we said they couldn't send him home because there was no one there to care for him. My sister and I had looked after Mom during

---

*Terms appearing in bold italics are defined in Chapter 8, "Who Pays"

this period, but eventually we had to get back to our jobs.

I contacted an ombudsman for hospitals and nursing homes affiliated with the state's office on aging. We notified the hospital of the action we had taken and they decided to transfer Daddy to a nursing home where he would receive therapy.

I also called the Inland Counties Resource Center for brain-impaired adults, which is a program mandated by the state, and spoke with a counselor there. Barbara Wilson talked me through my anxieties and helped prepare me to deal with "the system." She gave me language and words to use to get information from hospital staff and doctors.

After Dad's admittance to the nursing home, his doctor instructed me to get letters from him declaring both my parents mentally incompetent. These letters have helped us prove to the bank, and other agencies, that we need to handle my parents' affairs for them.

Although my sister and I had given the hospital and the nursing home our home phone numbers, we weren't notified when Dad suffered the second stroke after being transferred to the nursing home. Ironically, because Dad was now listed as "unstable," his **Medicare** would last longer. Still, his physician advised me to start the paper work for **Medi-Cal** on both my parents.

His physician also told me to expect the worst—that Dad probably would have another stroke and didn't have long to live. My sister and I decided that it would be better if Dad were cared for at home around familiar surroundings and with my mother.

From that point on we began tapping agencies that we thought could help us get home care, and our search led us to In-Home Supportive Services (IHSS), through the Department of Social Services. They provided the funds for a live-in caregiver for Mom immediately and for Dad when he got home from the hospital. The caregiver would be paid through **Medi-Cal**, supplemented by my parents own income, which consisted of approximately $1,100 monthly from social security and a small retirement.

During the first two weeks after my father's stroke, my sister and I were completely frustrated. Even if you know a little bit about the "system," it's tough to get help. We were lucky to get the kind of help we wanted for my parents.

According to a 1989 report from the Older Women's League, "Forty-two states fund limited home care services, including respite care and homemaker and personal care services, through a waiver program under **Medicaid**. However, all these programs combined serve only 100,000 elderly and disabled Americans. ...Meanwhile, one million seriously disabled elderly living at home receive no assistance at all."

It's easier to find and utilize sources of help if your parent has been discharged from a hospital that provides referrals. Depending on the expertise of the hospital staff, the referrals may range from free state or local services to cost-effective or expensive private-enterprise sources. If the hospital staff isn't up-to-date on available services or if the physician doesn't take the time to pass on information, the family is left on its own, often in an unfamiliar environment, to locate needed help.

If the elderly are at home and haven't been placed in the hospital first, finding such services can be even more difficult. Additionally, the services may not be covered under **Medicare** or by the supplemental insurance many elderly buy thinking it will cover long-term care.

My family is fortunate to live in California which, along with Florida, leads the nation in the services available for the aged because of their large elderly populations. Some states offer little or no assistance. However, as the shortage of care for the elderly is increasingly brought to public attention, more states are starting to offer creative solutions. For example, Wisconsin has initiated a "Community Option Program" that hires housekeepers, nurses, food services and senior-citizen volunteers for those who need help in the home. They provide these services for free or at minimal cost. Through the program we tapped into here in California, a case worker evaluates the condition of the one to receive care and funding is based on the types of services needed.

Be aware that communities vary in the services offered, and they go by different names. If you don't have a telephone book for the area in which your parent lives, begin by calling your state unit on aging (check the "Resources" guide in the back of this book). They will refer you to your local area agency on aging, and other agencies that could be helpful.

You might also check with your parent's local church for assistance or information. If the person being cared for has previously been hospitalized, check with the hospital's social service department and the physician's office.

If you feel unable to work through the system, or if you are trying to supervise care for your parent from another state, you may prefer to hire a care management agency to do the planning for you. Geriatric case or care management is a new business, which assists families in determining where and how to get help for an elderly relative. It's a good source even if the parent needing help lives near you.

An initial evaluation may cost approximately $300, but these agencies may save you money in the long run. And, most of the work can be handled by phone if the agency is a good one. These managers often come from a background of social work or nursing, and they know how to tap into the systems offered in the area where the elderly parent lives. Information on the National Association of Private Geriatric Care Managers is listed in the "Resources" section at the end of this book.

Home Assistance or Home Care

Services that can be provided in the home depend upon the person's condition. Unless they require hospitalization or constant monitoring, they can often stay fairly independent with home-health aides, nursing and/or physical therapy when needed, speech and hearing therapy, nutrition counseling, laboratory services, dental care, medical equipment and supplies, and some social services.

Home-health-care services are provided through both profit and nonprofit private agencies, public health departments and through hospitals.

Information about home-health agencies can be obtained from hospital social workers, local public health and welfare departments, agencies on aging, the United Way, through churches and synagogues, adult day-care centers, nursing institutions, the Social Security Administration, private physicians, the telephone directory and from support groups.

Skilled-nursing services required in the home are often reimbursable through **Medicare**, **Medicaid** and some private insurance plans. "Skilled nursing" is employed when the patient has specific medical needs—perhaps requiring intravenous medicines, various therapies and shots. If the patient simply needs help getting to the bathroom, eating, or being looked after because they suffer from dementia, funding is not usually available.

Connecticut Community Care Inc. (CCCI), established in 1974 as a government-funded pilot project, teaches agencies in other states how to provide home-care services for the elderly. It has grown into one of the largest and most successful independent agencies providing this service in the United States. It is also a care management agency.

"Studies show that people overwhelmingly prefer to get long-term care in the home," says Andrea Obston, spokesperson for CCCI. "We are the ombudsman for the elderly person. We act as a go-between for them and the community services, which can be very complicated. So what we do is not only say you need A,B,C, and D, but we walk you through the morass of stuff."

Obston likes to talk about Horace Hart who died last year at the age of 104 after having lived in his home up until three months before his death. "At the age of ninety-four, he'd been put in a nursing home and we got him out of there and he lived independently until just before he died. That's a dramatic case, but it's typical of the stories I hear."

Organizations such as the one in Connecticut not only assist the elderly with everything from legal services to housecleaning, but can help them develop long-term-care insurance. Initially, they evaluate what is needed, and then if the caregiver or elderly person desires, they will contract with the proper agencies to see that those services are delivered.

If the parent lives in another state, a care managing agency can be contacted in that area, the person's needs assessed, and at the direction of the caregiver, the agency will provide the needed service. The management service will even search out funds that might be available to provide the needed care. "A lot of people don't know these services exist. They say, 'Oh yeah, Meals on Wheels five days a week. What do we do the other two days?'" We have found grants that will pay the next door neighbor to serve meals. That's the kind of creativity we have," says Obston.

A similar program called Supportive Services Program for Older Persons (SSPOP) identifies and improves access to needed services for the elderly or their caregivers. The SSPOP program was funded by the Robert Wood Johnson Foundation, the nation's largest health care philanthropy, and is designed to be cost-effective. The services weren't meant to replace ones already provided through existing insurance, or the help given by family and friends, according to Russell Hereford, deputy director of the SSPOP. Rather, they are meant to fill in the gaps and provide services that would not otherwise be available. Once the programs are put into place with grant money from the Robert Wood Johnson Foundation, then they will serve as financially self-sufficient models for other agencies.

The medical aspects of caring for the elderly are often quite well taken care of by private health insurance and government programs. The objective of SSPOP is to provide help with the day-to-day, independent living concerns of the elderly and their caregivers, according to Hereford. The costs of these services vary widely because they are privately funded.

The types of services provided by SSPOP include:
- Case management
- Resource directory
- Caregivers and family counseling
- Respite for caregiver
- Personal assistance

- Personal affairs management
- Transportation
- Home delivered meals
- Housekeeping/cleaning
- Home delivered groceries/drugs
- Yard chores and upkeep
- Snow removal
- Emergency-response devices
- Health screening
- House inspections
- Major home repairs

A listing of eleven SSPOP centers is provided in the back of the book.

Visiting Nurses Associations (VNAs)

VNAs throughout the country began expanding home-care programs nearly twenty years ago, and today they provide patients with services that would normally have required hospitalization such as therapy, nutrition, social services and medication supervision. VNAs often cost more than some other agencies because they provide "skilled" nursing care, but they do accept **Medicare** and **Medicaid**.

Programs such as Connecticut Community Care, Inc. and Supportive Services Program for Older Persons, are only a few of the new types of services being offered throughout the United States. As the demand for inexpensive elder care increases, the cost of some of these services may become reimbursable through private insurance and **Medicare**. In the meantime, however, only those individuals who meet specified eligibility requirements can receive financial assistance, and then only if the agency helping them has received special funding for that purpose.

Assisted-Living Home Insurance

Another type of home-care assistance now emerging is Assisted-Living Home Insurance, which provides sources geared to help the elderly continue to live independently.

Health care professionals Anne Griffin and Lynn Goldis are working on a project called Life-Care-at-Home, an insurance protection plan that will provide programs for the elderly comparable to those given in continuing care retirement communities. Life-Care is only one of several hundred such programs in the developmental stages throughout the country. But it will give you an idea of how people are beginning to view the care of the elderly.

"The original concept of Life-Care was to develop a lower cost alternative to expensive retirement communities," says Griffin. "It was meant to offer all the same services but to allow the elderly to remain independent and at home." Premiums for the program will be age-banded—that is, the younger the person brought into the program, the less expensive it will be. Griffin estimates that Life-Care-At-Home will average about $200 per month if a person is brought into it at age sixty-five. The program will provide personal care attendants, chore workers, home delivered meals, transportation to adult day-care centers or physical therapy, and other live-at-home services.

"People dread going to a nursing home. The suicide rate among the elderly has increased twenty-five percent in the last seven years, and I think older people don't want to live if what they envision for their life is a nursing home," says Griffin.

Some of the major insurance companies are investigating the possibilities of offering this type of case-management insurance in the face of the increasing elderly population and the determination of people to stay independent as long as possible, according to Griffin.

Contact your local insurance agent for information on this type of insurance, or contact the Health Insurance Association of America (listed in the "Resources" section at the end of this book).

Adult Day-Care Centers

One of the most successful ways to assist caregivers appears to be adult day-care centers. Approximately fifteen hundred of them have sprung up across the country in little more than ten years and more are emerging because of their proven success. Adult day-care centers lift the burden of those caring for elderly parents in their homes. They can be used during the day by caregivers who have jobs and are also helpful as respite care for those who stay home full time with an aged parent. Adult day-care centers are mostly used by people who must continue working and who can't care for their elderly parents during the day, and by caregivers who need to get away for awhile.

Those attending adult day care are usually women past the age of seventy with an average monthly income of less than $500. Half of them need some form of supervision, with about twenty percent needing constant supervision. Nearly ten percent of them are incontinent and require changing during the day and another ten percent are developmentally disabled. Twenty percent of them use a walker or cane and about eight percent use a wheelchair.

Adult day-care centers may be emerging as a place to enrich the lives of the elderly because of the activities that are often offered. Many of these centers, rather than being a place to take someone to sit in front of a TV all day, offer activities ranging from art to outings.

Senior Service Corporation, provider of services and products for senior citizens (day-care centers among them), has initiated a joint venture with Holiday Inn whereby the elderly are offered such activities as swimming, art and skills therapy, exercise, beauty parlor and barber services, and personal care and hygiene (see "Resources").

Senior Service Corporation's president, Maurice Thompson, a millionaire entrepreneur, became interested in care for the elderly through the experiences of his own parents. During the time his mother was dying of congestive heart failure and his father was deteriorating with Alzheimer's disease, he felt inadequate because he couldn't find the type of care that he was seeking. Thompson says he was "galled" by the lack of affordable care-facilities for his parents, and by attitudes that lacked compassion in the treatment of the elderly. "A person of any age deserves dignity," he says.

He points out that it costs approximately $35,000 a year to keep an elderly person in a nursing facility and believes the country will have to start paying attention to other alternatives, especially if those alternatives offer the elderly a better lifestyle.

Fortunately, day care is catching on. Forty-two states now regulate adult day care, but it is wise to check out the center in your area before placing your parent in their care. Things to look for in choosing a center include:

1. Whether it is certified or licensed, and if it has adequate medical staff who can give first aid, such as CPR.
2. What types of activities are provided, and whether there is an extra charge for the special activities or if it is included in the initial fee.
3. What the policies and procedures to use in an emergency are and the means to make complaints.
4. If the meals provided are healthful and if special diets can be accommodated.

The average cost of day care is $30 per day. Federal and state assistance is sometimes available for adult day care, and often staff at day-care centers know how to tap these and other sources for financial help. Also, some insurance companies will reimburse a portion of the expenses, especially if it defrays nursing home costs.

Legislation has been introduced on the national level to reimburse day-care costs through **Medicare**. Proponents of the bill believe it will assist in forestalling families from placing the elderly in nursing homes because it will enable them to continue working and leading a more normal life. They believe it will be cost-effective.

The state agencies that oversee adult day-care centers are listed in the "Resources" section at the end of this book.

Telephone Networking and Reassurance

Many volunteer organizations such as churches and civic agencies provide daily contact for homebound individuals. The client calls in every day at a specified time, or the volunteer or caseworker calls the client. If contact isn't made, a neighbor or the police are alerted. Some areas provide visitors to the home, similar to the telephone program.

These services, though they seem simple, add reassurance to an older person. If the parent is still living alone, the adult child could call in once or twice a day if they can't look in on the person. Or they can contact a local volunteer organization to see if they provide such services.

There are more sophisticated phone services being initiated. A high-tech communication system called

Care-Line brings small groups of caregivers together who talk to one another on the phone in a rotating pattern. It was originally set up as a demonstration project by the University of Southern California Andrus Gerontology Center, and only persons who provide care at home for a family member suffering from Alzheimer's participated in the pilot project.

The network was designed to help caregivers who can't get out of the home to get in contact with other caregivers who are also homebound. They may be too frail to attend support group meetings or may not be able to arrange for someone to come into the house and care for the person while they attend a support group meeting. Also, in some areas, there are no established support groups. Catherine Goodman, one of the program's directors, said the program is particularly useful to those who are geographically dispersed and can't attend support group meetings.

"We had one woman whose marriage was about to break up because she was so run-down taking care of an elderly relative," recalls Goodman. "The phone program allowed her to vent her feelings with someone." Through the project, participants are able to find emotional support as well as practical advice on how to cope with the changes in their lives. As one woman in the program said, "I have friends, but they don't realize what I'm going through." She also says that some of her longtime friends have gradually lost contact as her husband's Alzheimer's has progressed because it's hard on them seeing him the way he is. Also, many of the couple's older friends aren't well themselves.

Goodman believes that Care-Line's network model could be easily and inexpensively used by a variety of other agencies and organizations to assist caregivers.

The Care-Line pilot project also studied the effectiveness of giving tapes of expert opinions to caregivers on such topics as what Alzheimer's is and how it acts, legal and financial aspects of the disease, how to care for the person with Alzheimer's, medications, and tips on nursing home placement.

Peter Braun, executive director of the Alzheimer's and Related Disorders Association in Los Angeles, which coordinates about fifty Alzheimer's support groups, says that the Los Angeles chapter is going to put the Care-Line concept into use.

Other options for elder care that have been gaining a foothold in our country are **HOUSE SHARING**, whereby two or more elderly people share the costs of sustaining an independent household. You can obtain information on this procedure by contacting your state unit on aging and getting referral numbers for agencies in your, or your parent's, area that may have such programs. Not all areas have them.

BOARD-AND-CARE HOMES, with an average cost of $700 per month, are usually privately operated facilities that assist the elderly by providing a room, meals, some personal care services and around-the-clock protection. Not all states license, or even monitor, board-and-care facilities.

In some areas, local governments, religious organizations or other nonprofit groups have established

SENIOR-HOUSING FACILITIES that provide rooms with central dining, social and recreational programs and minor health services. This type of housing varies in cost from less than $100 a month to several hundred, depending on the funding available to the organization, and on the senior's income. These nonprofit facilities generally have waiting lists.

CONTINUING-CARE RETIREMENT COMMUNITIES offer some of the best services available, but the initial fees can range from approximately $20,000 to $400,000, with monthly costs of $400 to $2,000. Buying into one of these communities should be done with caution. Most are quite reputable, but some have run into financial difficulty, gone through bankruptcy and been abandoned. Many seniors have lost life savings in this manner. Scrutinize the contract carefully, and seek the advice of an attorney before signing any contracts.

INFORMAL SUPPORT SYSTEMS can include neighbors, a church and local county or city programs. These sources can offer such programs as telephone reassurance whereby clients call in daily, or a volunteer calls the client to make certain everything is OK. These same informal sources sometimes provide visitor programs that check on the elderly person on a daily or weekly basis.

MEALS-ON-WHEELS, which has been in place for several years, delivers hot meals, once or twice daily, five days a week. It not only provides reassurance of proper nutrition for your parent, but at the same time provides a personal checking system on them. The cost is nominal, and is based on a sliding-fee scale.

A new program called Interfaith Volunteer Caregivers is being tried in more than 125 communities nationwide. It organizes participating religious congregations to serve the elderly population with friendly visits, transportation, in-home help, and referral to other relevant community services. For those interested in obtaining more information on this program, contact the National Federation of IVC, Inc. listed in "Resources" in the back of this book.

Support Groups

When my sister, Theda, and I were getting ready to leave for our own homes after several days at my parent's, she said, "Well, I guess when I get home, I'll call Linda. That always helps." Linda is a neighbor and close friend of my sister's who cared for her mother-in-law in her home until the older woman died recently. She has been through the entire experience first hand. While Linda was providing that care she frequently used to slip over to my sister's place and cry on her shoulder. "It gave her a place to let down and get rid of some of her frustrations," Theda recalls. Now Theda is leaning on Linda.

Most of the time, however, caregivers feel alone. They believe they are the only ones experiencing such intense feelings. But they aren't alone. Nearly every state provides support groups of one sort or another and for the most part, the groups are effective. Sources that may have information about support groups are local hospitals, senior centers or your area agency on aging. Also, many states have clearinghouses that provide information about all types of self-help groups (see listing in "Resources" in the back of this book).

Studies conducted at several universities indicate that people who get support and those who have more information about the caregiver's role stay healthier; that men and women differ on the reasons for stress during caregiving (men are more influenced by the degree of impairment of the one being cared for, and women are more influenced by their social support and amount of work involved); and that the caregiver's stress can be related to other aspects of life and not just directly to the caregiving role. Also, when the caregiver has a positive relationship with the one being cared for, when he or she feels competent in the job and is allowed time to pursue other interests and relationships, he or she is better able to withstand the caregiving load. Yet, studies show that most caregivers don't seek help until the situation has reached a crisis point.

❤   ❤   ❤

The programs discussed in this chapter have sprung up as more humane and cost-effective alternatives to an outmoded and antiquated system of taking care of the elderly. These new programs will pave the way for established networks of help for tomorrow's caregivers. But since we are on the cutting edge of this transition from the institutional thinking of yesterday to the homebound ideas of today, nothing is laid out for us.

Some of us live in areas where these programs aren't yet in place. That proverbial point of entry is, as yet, elusive. We have to design the road maps ourselves. And sometimes it's OK to become angry at a system that seems to fail us when we need it.

Major problems seem to arise when you must take over completely for parents, have done no previous planning, and are thrown into an unfriendly and overworked system. Unfortunately, this is what happened to my sister and I. We were led from one agency to another, and to physicians so tied up in the system that they didn't have time to return our calls. Each time we went to my parents' home to take care of more business, we left exhausted. Fortunately, we're both fighters and we've filed complaints, gotten hearings and are slowly getting problems ironed out.

Even if circumstances are better for some than they were for us, most adult children who become responsible for their parents are not only dealing with a bureaucracy, but are involved in the situation emotionally, financially and personally. They are dealing with other family members, neighbors and friends of their parents as well as their own issues.

My sister and I were never close in the past, but we are finding out that we share similar views on some of the major life and death issues that we face. We call one another more frequently than ever before. Usually it's to vent some frustration, and once that's done, we laugh about a few things and console ourselves about the good things that are happening in a macabre situation.

For one thing, Mama finally got some psychiatric treatment for the depression that had plagued her since she was diagnosed with Alzheimer's. In lucid moments, she's aware and able to talk about her disease.

Daddy was in his own home surrounded by the familiar things he loved. His speech had improved, he was able to get around a little bit more and we saw the fight he put up.

My sister and I will continue to encourage change and reform in this country's fragmented system of elder care. And we'll continue to tap every source available to ensure a high quality of life for my mother and for us.

Getting the Best Nursing Care 4

ONE IN FOUR PERSONS past the age of sixty-five will spend some time in a nursing home. If you have been caring for your parent, either in your home or overseeing their care at their residence or in some other type of interim facility, the decision to place them in a nursing home doesn't mean you are deserting them. The caregiving responsibilities continue, and, often, families don't relinquish their caregiving roles, physically or emotionally. Placement in a nursing home usually means that the son or daughter is simply unable to care for the person any longer. Or, many times, the parent will be placed in a nursing facility on the advice of a physician following a severe illness or a hospital stay.

It's a myth that sons and daughters put their parents into nursing homes because they don't want the responsibility of caring for them. Most adult children have exhausted themselves emotionally and physically before they consider a nursing facility. A study by Connecticut Community Care, Inc. found that people spend an average of forty months taking care of their older relatives before they turn to a nursing home.

It may be time to consider a nursing facility for your loved one when:

- They become chronically incontinent
- Their care interferes with your own family life, creating serious conflict with your spouse or children
- It is affecting your own health
- The elderly person becomes a danger to themselves or others (wandering, starting fires)
- Their health demands continuing nursing care

There are several types of nursing facilities available. Skilled-nursing homes provide nursing service on a twenty-four-hour basis for convalescent patients. Other types of nursing facilities are residential-care facilities that offer supervised living accommodations to people who are still capable of functional independence; and intermediate-care facilities that provide room and board, and some medical, nursing, social and rehabilitative services to the elderly who aren't capable of full independent living. There is also mental health care for those who suffer mental illness and who are in need of long-term care.

Dread of nursing homes stems from the historical origins of the almshouses of Colonial America, which served as the first institutions for our nation's old and sick. Called "poorhouses" in the 1920s, they were eventually forced out of existence by public outrage because of their deplorable conditions. The Social Security Act of 1935 paved the way for private, for-profit boarding homes in which the residents could continue to receive their federal old-age benefits (seniors couldn't receive social security if they were in a public institution). These boarding homes eventually became our present day nursing and convalescent homes. They were regulated in the 1950s. But the onus of the original almshouses has stayed with them.

Sister Margaret Mary, administrator of Marycrest Manor in Culver City, California, believes the public needs to be enlightened about nursing homes in our society. Nursing homes are needed and only a minority of them aren't doing the job right. Sometimes they are absolutely necessary for the peace of mind of families involved with an elderly person. In many cases, families keep the elderly one at home too long until the stresses become unbearable for the family, says Sister Margaret Mary, one of the early pioneers in the hospice movement in London.

"The children of these people needing placement reach a point where they can't care for them anymore and they always suffer a little bit of guilt when they put them in a nursing home. I explain to people that they must not feel guilty because they can't cope with mom. They must not feel guilty, because they are doing the best they can. I tell them not to be surprised if they feel terrible on the day they bring their parent here. They may have a guilt trip. Maybe even an added one put on by mother."

Even after placement, the guilt will continue often because of the parent. "We had a wonderful old lady here and every time her daughter came, the mother gave the daughter a terrible guilt trip. The daughter would come by to see me in tears and I would tell her that her mom was doing it deliberately. I told her her mother was happy here. That she eats her meals and takes part in all the activities. But when the daughter came, the mom got angry and took it out on her. I told the daughter, 'Don't let her do that to you. You'll be talked into taking her home and you can't.'"

We are frightened to place our parents in a nursing home because we've all heard and read horror stories about neglect and even brutality, in a few of them. The truth is, however, there is more elder abuse in the home setting than in nursing homes. Many elderly are abused by their caregivers and conversely, many caregivers are tyrannized by the people they are caring for. The Pepper Committee on Aging estimates that 3.6 percent of the nation's elderly are abused by caregivers each year. It's expected to get worse due to the growth of the elderly population and the stress placed on those caring for them. If the condition of the older person worsens, or if a particular family member has a history of violence, the chances of abuse increase.

Many adult children provide care because they feel obligated to do so and not because they want to, according to a study by W. Strawbridge and M. Wallhagen.

However, their parents often feel that their children should not have to provide care. Also, the study indicates that family relationships improve after nursing home placement.

On the other hand, abuse in nursing homes is being addressed. There are studies being conducted on it, new regulations being implemented to improve care in the nation's fifteen thousand nursing homes, and several advocacy groups monitoring nursing home care.

The bottom line is: the more money spent on nursing home care, the better that care is. As Sister Mary Margaret explains, a quality nursing home costs the patient about $36,000 per year. Quality of care also depends on the ratio of professional caregivers to patients. In some nursing facilities, the ratio of nurses to patients is one to fifteen, and this sets the stage for abuse because caring for that many patients puts a professional caregiver under too much stress.

"Every old person should be entitled to good care in nice surroundings with caring people," says Sister Margaret. "A person may be very caring but doesn't have the time. They're under a great deal of stress, and get burned out quickly. Nurses are difficult to come by right now. There is a tremendous shortage throughout the country, and on the whole, nurses don't want to work in nursing homes. Working in a nursing home is not as prestigious as working in a well-known hospital.

"The patient in a nursing home may be a cranky old lady. She may be combative. No one is grateful—not the patient and not the family. In nursing homes, the patient doesn't usually get well so the family doesn't look on the staff in gratitude for saving the person's life," Sister Margaret says. She believes that the public has to change its attitudes toward the staff at nursing homes. "One patient may be the sweetest old darling and say thank you, but the next is cranky. Nothing the nurse does pleases her. It wears down the nurse. Then, the lady complains to the family and the family comes in and they listen to mother. Sometimes the family forgets that mom used to complain at home and they blame the nurse. 'Why didn't the nurse do this or that? My mother says this or that.' So the nurse gets blamed for all sorts of things and she gets depressed." Furthermore, some family members may still feel guilty about placing Mom or Dad in the nursing home, so they take it out on what they perceive as negligence on the part of the staff, Sister Margaret says.

However, some of the negligence in nursing homes may be a result of poor work conditions and underskilled workers. A study by V. Tellis-Nayak and Mary Tellis-Nayak of the University of Illinois, found that nurses aides, who account for about seventy-one percent of the nursing staff at nursing facilities, often come from backgrounds of poverty and adversity. They are among the least educated, skilled and paid in the health care labor market. "From such a setting, the nurse's aide enters the nursing home and may find that in many ways, both subtle and overt, the home compounds her problems, erodes her fragile optimism and hardens her attitude," the Tellis-Nayak's study reports. It also calls for new policies that respect the social, psychological and organizational needs of the aides.

Given all these problems, you may feel overwhelmed when faced with placing your parent in a nursing home. But it's not an impossible task to find a good facility. One of the first things to check is the ratio of nursing staff to patient, Sister Margaret says. One staff member to eight patients is an average.

Staff should be willing to provide you with any information requested, including the latest inspection report as required by the state. Family members should, on request, be given a complete tour of the facilities, including the kitchen and laundry facilities.

While on the tour you should take note of:

- Cleanliness of the facility
- Lighting
- Room space and accommodations
- Atmosphere
- Noise level

Your personal needs and those of other family members should be considered. These considerations might include:

- Closeness of facility to the majority of family members
- Flexible and adequate visiting hours
- Whether you are allowed to join your parent for a meal and for a reasonable cost
- If children are welcome

Ask if the home provides any special services, such as:

- Dental services
- Physical, speech or occupational therapy
- Special diets
- Special programs such as dancing, exercise or music
- Counseling
- Religious services or clergy rounds

Other considerations:

- Does the facility allow treatment by the physician of your parent's choice?
- What are the procedures for airing your grievances?
- Are the rooms cheerful and comfortable?
- Are meals tasty and served at the proper temperature?
- Is a pleasant outdoor area available?
- Is there a lounge?
- Are there extra charges for laundry, snacks, or bringing in a private TV?
- Does the nursing home provide a list of additional costs and fees on demand?

Many nursing homes have family councils or groups that meet at specific times with staff to air grievances and offer ideas for helpful changes, future activities, and in some cases, to act as mutual support meetings. Marge N. of Virginia, whose mother is in a nursing home, says the councils offer a lot of strength to family members and that a person can get as active as they desire.

Another major factor to consider in choosing a nursing facility is whether or not it allows the patient to die in that facility without transfer to a hospital, or whether at the slightest emergency, the patient is sent to the hospital. In most states, it is law that unless otherwise legally stipulated in a **living trust, living will,** a **durable power of attorney for health care** or certain types of **conservatorships,** a dying patient will be placed on life-support systems once transferred to a hospital. It will be mostly your decision (unless your parent made his or her wishes known), whether or not to select a nursing home such as the one administered by Sister Margaret at Marycrest, that allows the patient to die peacefully in bed with family members around them.

"Once they're on life-support, it's the devil to get them off legally," says Sister Margaret. "When I first came here it was against the law to let anyone die. The lives of the dying were prolonged so God couldn't have His way. We used to have to stick them on life-support and I would ask the inspectors, 'Who gave you the right to say, "Don't go to God when your time's up," and who gave you the right to keep them here and torture them?'

"The dying person should be comfortable, pain-free and have all the tender loving care you can give him or her. We had a woman die here the other day. She died peacefully with her daughter holding her head in her lap."

Laws vary in individual states. Sometimes the decision to place a person in a hospital will be the doctor's. "We had a lady here about two months ago who went to the hospital because the doctor ordered it. She would have died here within a few hours if she had remained here. As it was, we had to send her to the hospital. They put her on life-support, she had to have a tracheotomy, surgery, they put a tube down in her stomach, she had needles all over her—IV's with medications going in, and she lasted five weeks.

"Our ethics and philosophies have got to catch up with our technology," declares Sister Margaret. "We're not talking about euthanasia here. We're talking about God's call." Sister Margaret and others believe this tender loving care would be easier to give if things weren't so regulated by the state. "You feel like saying, I can't take it any longer. Why don't we give this up altogether. It's almost impossible to give tender loving care with some of these outrageous regulations. They are made by people with good intentions, but they really don't know what they're talking about. They are courting votes. So they sponsor a bill that looks good because it appears to crack down on nursing homes. If a nursing home is inadequate because of inadequate funding, how do you cure the situation by going in and giving them a $25,000 fine?"

A source of empowerment for the elderly in dealing with their health and care is the ombudsman program. Every state is required to provide the public with an ombudsman who serves as an advocate to help resolve complaints made on behalf of nursing home and hospital residents. My sister and I used the services of an ombudsman when my father's insurance company was planning to send him home from the hospital to the care of my mother. With the help of the ombudsman, my father was placed in an interim facility for therapy.

The ombudsman program grew out of the Older Americans Act, which enforces the rights of the elderly in the United States. Many states provide *local* ombudsmen who are readily available to help families with their problems. In some states, programs exist where volunteers work with the ombudsman's office to regularly visit nursing homes for information inspections.

Also, the federal government has recently enacted two bills of rights for nursing home residents—one for skilled-nursing facilities and one for intermediate-care facilities.

These bills stipulate that nursing facilities must inform patients of:

- the facilities' rules and regulations
- the services available and any related charges
- their medical condition
- their right to participate in decisions about medical treatment
- their right to reasonable advance notice of transfer or discharge
- their right to air grievances without reprisal
- their right to manage personal financial affairs

These bills also assert that patients' rights include:

- confidential treatment of personal and medical records
- private visits for married couples, or a shared room if both are patients

- ❤ freedom from mental and physical abuse
- ❤ freedom from chemical or physical restraints unless authorized in writing by a physician
- ❤ freedom to send and receive personal mail and communicate privately with persons of their choice
- ❤ freedom to participate in all activities in the facility as desired
- ❤ freedom to have personal clothing and possessions as space permits

Copies of these bills, including additional rights enacted by individual states, can be obtained from your state's ombudsman by contacting your area's agency on aging or from your hospital or nursing facility ombudsman. Sometimes, senior citizen groups can also provide copies of these bills.

When I first began looking for my particular state agency on aging, I didn't know where to begin since each state has adopted its own title and in some cases is linked to existing agencies. Therefore, when looking in the phone book, you might have to look under Aging and Adult Services, Office on Aging, Division of Aging, etc. State agencies administering the Older American's Act are listed in the back of this book, under "State Units on Aging." They can also provide information on your state's ombudsman office.

❤   ❤   ❤

You, as the primary caregiver, will have to make some of the decisions on how your parent's final years are to be spent. These won't be easy decisions, and making them takes a certain amount of toughness. These decisions don't just encompass what we want for our parents because what we want is sometimes different than the reality. But we can aim in the direction of "wants." In the perfect scenario, I would have wanted my parents to live out their lives in a home setting with my sister and I by their sides. When it was time for them to die, I would have wanted them in their own beds with their family around them. The reality is that I must work full time to support myself. My home is a three-hour drive away from theirs. I knew I would be incapable of tending to their physical needs, such as lifting my father. My sister felt much the same way. There is only so much she can do because of her business, her health and the long distance to our parents' home.

What my sister and I did to obtain some of our "wants" was to start the process for getting my parents on **Medi-Cal** and to get the full-time caregiver, paid mostly through **Medi-Cal**. My dad improved tremendously after coming back to his own home. His speech returned and he started to use his right hand.

Whatever happens next, we will deal with it. We know you can't sit back and let the system take over. It doesn't work that way. The system reminds me of a dragon. You simply have to go out and slay it.

It also helps to step back and look at the reasons why the health care system is seemingly cold and uncaring. It's easier to get some perspective on your own predicament when you remember that the health care system is in crisis, that people working in the system are frequently overworked and burdened, and that it is impossible for someone else to feel the pain you might be feeling over your aging parent.

Making 5
Peace With
the Family

SHIRLEY E.'S GARDEN IS LUSH with crisp summer vegetables, so much so that she's continually giving the bounty to neighbors—all this despite its being her first attempt ever to garden.

She says it's the only thing that helps her maintain her sanity. She's trying to balance the amount of time she gives to her father and mother who were divorced several years ago. Although she isn't taking care of either full time, both are homebound and ailing, and she helps them nearly every day with little chores like setting her mother's hair or shopping for her father.

Her husband resents the time she spends with her parents and believes it's infringing on their marriage. He's getting ready to retire and has been looking forward to doing some traveling.

Shirley's case is not that unusual. Actually, it's more the norm. We step into the role of caregiving amidst all sorts of conflicts. It never happens at an "easy" time in our lives.

It would be great if all these life changes would happen to us when we're full of great self-esteem, have a pretty good idea of what lies ahead, know how to work the system and get the right help, have plenty of money with which to work and have parents with whom we get along. It helps too if our spouses and children are helpful and understanding, and if there are no conflicts with brothers and sisters. But life isn't perfect and circumstances are rarely so ideal.

When we first begin to realize that our parents need help, we start working our way through a labyrinth of conflicting emotions and hurdles that are put in our paths. Chief among them are unresolved conflicts with our parents—nagging leftovers from childhood like the bread crusts we used to leave underneath our plates. Therefore, one of the best beginnings is to make peace with our parents and with other family members long before a crisis with our aging parents begins.

Stepping into the role of a caregiver is tough under the best of conditions, but it's nearly impossible when one has never gotten along with the person being cared for. And the task is made even tougher if problems haven't been settled with spouses or with other family members. Taking care of Mom or Dad often opens old wounds with siblings, and causes conflicts with spouses.

Harold H. Bloomfield, M.D., bestselling author of *Making Peace With Your Parents*, says if there are unresolved conflicts by the time a person steps into the role of caregiver, it's likely to end in disaster.

"It absolutely creates problems if they haven't made peace with their parents," he says. "Chances are that nearly everyone will, at some point, become caregivers. Our parents are living longer and most of us are going to be caught in the 'sandwich' generation—taking care of our own kids at the same time our parents start needing us. So it's all going to affect us financially as well as emotionally. So, if you resent them for something you felt they didn't do in the past, your feeling may be, 'Why should I now take care of you, you rotten so-and-so. Look what you did to me when I was a kid.'

"You're going to feel guilty about these thoughts because even as adults we have that hurt inner child that needs to make peace with the parents of our childhood."

Bloomfield knows from whence he speaks. It took him years to come to terms with his own parents, and not until his father was dying of cancer was he really able to understand why his parents had done some of the "crazy" things that had upset him for most of his life.

"One of the biggest hurdles to overcome is the 'approval trap,'" he says. "Regardless of how old children are, they still desire their parents' approval. We never have anyone's one hundred percent approval. So why should we expect it from our parents? You can live a thousand miles from your parents, but you are still tied to them. And for your own peace of mind, the unfinished business must be settled."

Bloomfield, like many of us, had harbored resentments against his parents until he finally decided to make peace. Instead of trying to change them, he simply changed his own attitudes about them and accepted them as they were. He came to realize that despite a wide gulf of differences between him and his parents, he had gotten many positive values from them such as the attitude that "wealth isn't everything," and the importance of commitment and integrity. His parents also taught him to love life, to respect all people, and that struggling for things is often worth the effort.

The outcome of making peace with his parents was that the tension that had nearly always existed between them disappeared. He eventually became better friends with his mother and was able to show and receive affection from his father who had never been the demonstrative type.

Bloomfield adds that making peace with your parents spills over into other relationships. "Taking care of a parent has huge implications. It's very important that it be a joint issue with your spouse. It simply won't work for one spouse to say, 'Well, if you want to take care of him or her, go ahead, but don't expect anything from me.' That would be an impossible situation. It really requires a full partnership, so it's important to have your spouse and kids, if they're still living with you, be a part of the decision making, rather than letting it be imposed on them."

If the caregiving is done out of guilt, the entire situation gets out of hand very rapidly. "I've seen marriages break up and children neglected over a parent brought into the household," says Bloomfield.

Part of the problem lies in not allowing the one being cared for to take a working part in the family. Bloomfield recommends that the one being cared for not simply sit back and receive but be allowed to "give" if they are capable of it. To this end, the caregiver should become acquainted with the parent's physician and discuss with them just how capable the parent is and what you can reasonably expect from them. Some caregivers expect too much from their elderly parents and others expect too little. Neither scenario gives the elderly person much dignity.

Many times it's difficult for us to see our parents as helpless in some situations. They've always been the strong ones and taken care of most things. "It's very hard to see this person whom we've looked to all our lives as the rock of stability, who was always going to be there, deteriorate, lose their mental capacities and slowly die," says Bloomfield.

But it's absolutely normal for us to feel these things. "Often times people go through grief, like wishing the person would die already. Then they feel guilty at those thoughts of not being able to stand being around them because it's so painful. They have episodes of intense anger and don't know what to do with it. You resent your parents being so dependent upon you, and often when a parent dies after a long chronic illness, it's a relief. And then the person feels guilty about that," Bloomfield adds.

Bloomfield believes it's of utmost importance for caregivers to realize they are going to have all sorts of emotions ranging from the love they feel for their parents, to denial to downright hate.

"The truth is, no matter what you do, no matter what you think, it's never enough. Your parents are going to get sick and they are going to die. So you've got to find out what works for you and quit beating yourself up," says Bloomfield.

Carol Vogel, forty-two-year-old mother of two grade-school age children says, "By making peace with parents when you're older, you find a different person there. They come to you as an equal. All of a sudden you start looking out for their welfare and you can become friends. I've seen things in my dad that were always there, but that I never saw as a child." Carol made peace with her father after a lifetime of family conflict and following the death of her mother and an only sister.

Her father was a depressive who hardly ever spoke to his wife or two daughters except to lecture them and put them down. "He was chronically depressed. So what happens in that state is that you cut yourself off and you're so into yourself that you cut others off. You can't listen to others. When you're unhappy and sad a lot, any interference—children, wife—is disruptive."

Carol understands her father's illness now. But as a child and young adult she knew nothing of it. Only that life at home was miserable. She ate many meals in her room just to avoid the gloom of eating with the family, and she left home as soon as possible and put herself through college, even though her parents assured her she'd never make it.

She found out when she was sixteen that her mother had been having an affair with a friend of the family. "Mom was living the junior prom all her life. She always felt a prince charming would take her away from all this. She needed the security of a man there. Her own father left her when she was seven.

"After my mom died all my anger came to a head and I blamed my father for it. I blamed him because when my sister was in the hospital, she wanted him to come see her and he never did.

"Looking back I couldn't have changed anything. I couldn't have made it better, but I saved myself from being pulled under."

Soon after her mother's death from cancer in 1985, her father sold the family home back East and moved to California, a few hundred miles from where Carol lived. "I remember my sister had told Dad that he was going to be a bitter, lonely old man some day if he didn't change. And as much as I had this anger toward my dad, there was a part of me that had empathy—not sympathy. I came to feel that his problems weren't only brought on by himself, but that his illness hadn't been helped by the environment we had lived in.

"He had never wanted children and he was married to a woman who felt that's what you did when you got married. She basically tricked him into having my sister and I was the result of a broken condom. His underlying theme was, 'I didn't want them in the first place. You had them, so you take care of them.'

"Anyway, I was thinking about him one Christmas being there all by himself, and then Easter came and I thought about him again, and I started thinking that well, he'd never hurt me physically. Emotionally he did. He made my sister and I feel unwanted. So one day, I decided to write him and tell him exactly how I felt." Carol poured out all her hurt, anger and doubts and admits it was a violent letter. A friend read it and told her not to send it, so she didn't.

"A year later I wrote another letter and instead of telling him all those hateful things that I thought, I apologized for whatever I had ever done or said to hurt him. He had learned to expect all this anger from me. I wrote a letter of apology. I knew he was getting older and all that was left was the two of us. I felt that family is family. I asked him, 'What is the point of us carrying all this anger when we both need one another?' I said how it would be nice if he would come out here and we could start over again and forget about the past because it was doing us no good."

They began corresponding after that, and then he moved to a senior citizen retirement center close to where Carol and her family live.

"He usually comes out on Sunday and I'll make a warm lunch—soup, chicken—and then we'll have a light meal at night. Then he goes back to his apartment.

He's never been close to my children, but he gives me advice about them. For the first time in his life, I think he is happy. He's clean, quiet, not meddlesome."

Ten years ago, Carol never thought she could be that close to her father. Now she says, "There is a real nice person there I can see. My father is really a very kind man who has been deeply hurt. But it was me who had to take the initial step to change my attitude. He would never have done it."

Bloomfield too says that the children usually have to take that first step. "No, your parents aren't going to take the first step to make peace with you. But what does it matter anyway? If you take the first step, you hold the power. The person who knows they have the power is the person who takes responsibility for that power."

He advises children, whether or not they are caring for their parents, to be accepting of their parents' values, understand their point of view and try to be gentle with them rather than combative. "You're not going to change them," he says, "and if you continue the war, no one wins." Like it or not, it's the children who must change—not their lives, not their own value system and not their own philosophies, but their attitudes toward their parents.

Bloomfield points out that nearly all children, regardless of their ages, have "unfinished business" with at least one of their parents. He adds that many people fail to see how fundamental their relationships are with their parents and that all the feelings we associate with them still exist—ones that influence our own family lives, our sexuality, our political ideas, our ideas of pleasure and work, and how we get along with others.

"The more elderly parents are included in decision making and the more everyone talks about how they feel, the more there is going to be openness. Otherwise you get a situation where everyone is trying very hard for everything to go perfectly and it's like walking on egg shells and waiting for an explosion," he says.

For some of us, taking care of an elderly parent is a return to our worst nightmare. It's like going back to the prison of our childhoods. The parent is telling you what to do and what not to do. It's crucial in this situation to come to terms with your parent and establish a more open relationship in which feelings can be discussed, if the arrangement is to work.

If you're having problems with a parent who is trying to run your life again, Bloomfield suggests you say something like, "Mom, Dad, I want you to know that you can have input, but I'm an adult and will be making my own decisions and I don't need you telling me how to live my life. In regards to your own well-being, however, you're going to be participating as much as possible in whatever decisions we're going to make."

In addition to strained relationships with parents, many of us have to contend with sibling rivalry as well. It's the old thing of who is the caregiver among siblings. There are four distinct types of caregivers. If one doesn't understand the other, it can cause family feuds that will last a lifetime. These four primary types are:

❤ The head caregiver. This person often surfaces automatically, much like natural leaders in any group. They're frequently the oldest sibling.

❤ The one who gets off scot-free. Sometimes this person simply isn't capable of caring for the parent and arouses the resentment of other siblings who don't understand why.

❤ The one who's willing to put in a few dollars, but not the time. They might help out by hiring someone to clean the parent's home or to stay with them for the weekend instead of doing it themselves. Their attitude is often, "So what, as long as the help is there?" These people may have serious issues with their parents that haven't been worked out.

❤ The one who's still looking for Mom and Dad's approval and who often becomes a martyr. If they haven't taken over as the primary caregiver, they might complain about the one who has.

With an awareness of these different types of caregivers, it's easier to accept and accommodate sibling differences. It's also important to get your own needs met and to not get into the trap of being the only one who does any of the work and caring. If your parent has moved into your home, your concerns must be made clear to the parent and to your siblings.

❤ ❤ ❤

Joyce Colony of Charlottesville, Virginia, didn't realize she had conflicts with her parents until she established her own family.

She describes her mother as an "hysteric" who has had acute migraines, ulcers and other psychosomatic illnesses associated with the emotions, all of her life. Now, the mother is also suffering from the aftereffects of a stroke, osteoporosis, anorexia and short-term memory loss. She has always tried to control every situation and "the minute she's taken to the hospital, she starts bargaining and tries to throw guilt upon whoever will accept it."

The mother can't stand up without the help of a nurse, and can't always make it to the bathroom at night. The father is, as Joyce describes it, "comatose most of the time (not literally). But if you talk to him and penetrate that haziness, he's still as sharp as ever. He was a self-taught genius," she says.

For the time being, the mother refuses to move out of their home while her husband, who is partially deaf and blind, is still living. He is unable to provide any care because of his own frail health and they hire nursing care that costs up to $2,000 per month.

Joyce and her two sisters work together on how best to handle the situation and do so with the realization that there is a great deal of family anger. "But we realize we need each other and we're determined to be good friends," says Joyce.

"We've had eccentric parents all our lives. We just didn't realize how eccentric until we were grown up. For us, eccentricity was the norm."

Joyce recalls that her father went through a period of alcoholism, which left his liver permanently damaged, and that they were mostly left to fend for themselves when they were young because the mother isolated herself in the bedroom much of the time. A housekeeper was supposed to keep an eye on them, but never did so they fended for themselves. "We learned a lot about survival. We didn't realize we had to survive childhood. We were unsupervised most of the time, but it made it kind of a pleasant childhood. We were kind of unimpeded. No one telling us what not to do." For this reason, they won't tell their parents what to do now except to make sure they get the proper care at home.

"My parents live in horror of having to leave that house. It's the one we grew up in. My sisters and I decided that if that's what they want, it's their money and we'll do it as long as we can," says Joyce. Joyce's parents have lived in that house since they were married. "They have kept everything that has come through the doors in all those years. We've tried to clean some of it out already, but it angers my parents. They still live in fear of another Great Depression."

So the sisters are banding together to make the necessary decisions, and they're doing so with the realization that they must support each other to get anything accomplished.

Joyce laughs a lot when talking about the parents with whom she feels she has a love-hate relationship. "I heard Garrison Keillor once say that owning a harp was much like dealing with an elderly parent. They are difficult to get in and out of cars and very difficult to keep happy.

"I'm trying now to find a support group. I hope in Charlottesville there is such a group. I need to verbalize this. I can't keep talking to my husband and children about it. The minute anyone walks into the room, I'm ready to dump it on them, and I know I can't keep doing this."

Joyce isn't a novice at caring for the elderly. For six years she worked as a volunteer with hospice patients. "I know something about families, but it didn't prepare me for this. But my sisters and I are going to get through this. We are the best of friends. We have shrieking meetings. We laugh. We laugh because it's a release of tension. We talk about the money. How is this going to end up? Just what are we going to do for them? How are we going to feel when they go? I have clothes for a funeral, summer or winter. I mean, my mother has been dying since I was seventeen. If you don't have a sense of humor, you don't get through it."

Joyce met with her sister Betsy recently for a week's vacation. "On that first day we completed all our business and then had fun the rest of the time. We each have a file box that we keep all these records in so that at any given time we can confer by telephone. One keeps the household accounts—the day-to-day business; one keeps the health accounts—**Medicare**, Blue Shield; and another oversees the bank accounts and investments."

Joyce and her sisters' biggest hurt is over the fact that their parents always excluded them from their lives. "My mom and dad have always been in love with one another, and still are. Daddy doesn't see her as anything different than the girl he married. We were never allowed into their nucleus, and that's just the way it was. Mom lives in horror now that something will happen to her husband. She's furious that she might be left to take care of herself. If he leaves the room, a look of horror comes over her face," says Joyce.

"We could simply never abandon them. We needed them once and they were so powerful in our lives growing up. At one time, we couldn't believe that we could have existed without them. Now they can't live without us. Hopefully, we have matured enough to know that this is how families evolve," says Joyce, who firmly believes that her parents took care of them as best they could, despite shortcomings and trauma.

Still, Joyce realizes that problems that will never be resolved exist. "Betsy still can't stay overnight in the house because it brings back too much childhood pain. And it's exacerbated by the demands of these old people."

Joyce's sister, Carolyn, who lives closest to the parents in Roanoke, Virginia says, "My husband and I both feel that our parents are part of our family and caring for them is just something you do."

Carolyn's in-laws, in their eighties, also live nearby in nursing homes. The mother is suffering from Alzheimer's and the father from cancer, so Carolyn is serving double-duty. She is also the mother of two teens and a nine-year-old, and works part time. Her husband is a physician.

"We're very lucky that our children have known two sets of grandparents. Of course, since we live here in town we provide much of the practical support. Fortunately, both sides of the family pitch in to help." There is no problem with finances on either side of the family.

The circumstances of caring for our parents may vary, but we all have conflicts to settle, a lifetime of emotions to overcome, old hurts to forgive and let go of, and family dynamics to reconcile with, before we can become effective caregivers. When we can make peace with our parents and families, we can make peace with ourselves—a task that's not easy, but one we must accomplish to become complete and loving individuals.

Keeping Your Body and Spirit Healthy 6

MANY CAREGIVERS ARE SO INTENT on "doing the right thing" with the care of their parents that they neglect to look after themselves, even though they would be able to provide better care if they stayed in good physical and mental condition. There are ways of maintaining your health and sanity when caring for your parent. Not all are practical for everyone, but help is available if you just reach out. Research shows that the healthier the caregiver stays, the less likely they are to place their loved one in an institution.

Carolyn Lindgren, professor of nursing, says her interest in those caring for loved ones was piqued twenty-five years ago when, as a visiting nurse, she found that the caregiver frequently died before the one being cared for.

The level of caregivers' emotional exhaustion has been shown to be equal to that of professionals whose stress levels were scientifically measured at extremely high levels. Caregivers become physically and emotionally exhausted with good reason. Not only are the demands on their time and energy sapped with the care of loved ones, but they often lose established friendships; become sleep deprived; keep feelings of anger and hostility bottled up instead of acknowledging them as normal; feel trapped; suffer from chronic grief; are reluctant to seek outside help; and become excessively focused on caregiving.

Following are suggestions on how to escape some of these traps.

Loss of Established Friendships

Caregivers often lose established friendships because of demands on their time and because acquaintances feel uncomfortable around the one being cared for, especially if it involves a disease such as Alzheimer's, according to Sheila Bunting, M.S., of Wayne State University.

Most mental health professionals emphasize the importance of the caregiver staying in touch with friends and relatives, even if that contact is by phone. Caregivers can visit friends without their charges by establishing specific times to get away for awhile. This respite can be achieved by sharing the responsibility with other siblings. If you're the primary caregiver, insist that another member of the family relieve you one day a week. If that isn't possible, hire a sitter or take Mom or

Dad to a day-care center. If you don't have the funds to hire someone, ask for financial assistance from the brother or sister who doesn't have the time, or call your area agency on aging. They can often steer you to agencies that will help find financing for your respite care.

Many elderly people are willing to sit with someone for short periods of time and for minimal cost. It doesn't hurt to ask. Good places to look for sitters are churches, senior centers, an elderly neighbor, or a professional group, such as the Visiting Nurse's Association which sometimes supplies non-nursing professionals at less cost than that for nurses.

Support groups too can be utilized and they often provide care for the parent while the caregiver attends the group session. Support groups allow you to air your feelings with others who understand the situation.

It is also important to get away from talk of your caregiving problems. Find friends or acquaintances who can help lift the cloud of caregiving from your shoulders even for a brief period of sunshine.

I have called upon every friend whom I thought could be helpful, and they have been. When I was down because of my mom's temporary admittance to a psychiatric hospital and was getting little cooperation or information, a psychiatrist whom I had once done some work for called to give me an update on my mom's condition.

It was a breath of fresh air and he will be helpful in the future, both to my mom and to me. He was one of the few professionals we have dealt with who had any understanding or concern about the dynamics of the entire situation. He was one of the few to say to me, "You're holding up pretty good and doing a good job. Let me know if I can be of any help to you."

There are, as yet, few provisions in **Medicare** or private insurance to pay for hiring a sitter so the caregiver can get some respite. Nor do many of these policies pay for day care, although there are exceptions. Most professionals involved in caregiving issues believe that eventually **Medicare**, **Medicaid** and private insurance companies will help pay for respite care and day care because those agencies will realize the cost-effectiveness of keeping the caregiver healthy.

Loss of Needed Sleep

All too often the one being cared for is restless and wakes up at all times of the day and night depriving the caregiver of much needed sleep. "Sleep is a person's private time. The body and the psyche really need it, and it's nearly impossible for the caregiver in some cases to get enough sleep," says Lindgren.

Tips for getting this sleep include:

Regular exercise. If you are unable to get outside or go to a gym, equipment such as a stationary bicycle may help the situation. Videotapes can be used at specific times or some television stations offer exercise segments that you can join in on. Avoid strenuous routines just prior to bedtime. Some forms of yoga release tension, however, and can be used before going to bed. You might try getting your parent to join you in simple exercise routines. Consult with their physician first.

Muscle relaxation. While lying in bed, relax your toes, tighten and relax again. Proceed with this same routine of relaxation, tension and relaxation as you go up the body from the toes to the calves, to the thighs, the buttocks, the lower back, upper back and chest. Then continue the same routine at the shoulder, out to the arms, hands and the fingers. Next, concentrate on the neck, then the face and finally the head. During the tightening phase, tense the area strongly for fifteen to thirty seconds before relaxing.

To enhance the routine, inhale deeply and hold your breath when you tense your muscles and exhale slowly when you relax them. Also, you can try counting the seconds during the tension periods and visualizing your breath during the relaxation periods.

Visualization. Counting sheep, as long as you picture them lilting over the fence surrounded by a green pasture, and whatever else you might add to this peaceful scene, can enhance sleep.

If sleep problems persist, see a physician. Deprivation of sleep can cause major health and emotional problems. Lying awake at night and worrying about why you're unable to sleep only adds to the problem.

Feelings of Anger and Hostility

Caregivers have a lot of negative thoughts about the person they're caring for and then feel guilty about it, which is also bad for their health, Bunting says. "I want to emphasize that it's OK to have these feelings and OK at times not to like the one you're caring for," she says.

Caring for a loved one when the relationship has deteriorated often causes repressed fear and anger which in turn generates depression and feelings of guilt and hopelessness, according to Vernon Greene, director of the gerontology center at Syracuse University.

The truth is, if you have direct, hands-on, round-the-clock care of a parent, you have a right to all the feelings you're experiencing. Studies show that the psychological impact of caring for an elderly loved one is more debilitating than the physical work involved, such as lifting the person to remove a bedpan. Only a person who has experienced the demands of full-time care can fully understand the myriad of emotions you encounter during a twenty-four-hour period.

But you will harm yourself, and possibly the one you're caring for, if you don't acknowledge these emotions and deal with them. One of the best ways to deal with these angry feelings is to talk about them, either with a counselor or a friend. Humor can also help dissipate the anger. Learning to laugh at some of the seemingly horrible situations we as caregivers find ourselves in can help us get through many rough periods. "You'd think getting the person out of bed and cleaning them up would be the toughest thing to do. But studies have found that if you have a good mental attitude about it, it's not so hard," Bunting says.

Although most caregivers have fleeting moments of normal anger, those who are constantly angry at the entire situation may need professional help. Their anger is not normal for the situation and they need more extreme measures to deal with it.

Psychologist Joseph Becker of the University of Washington, says that people who have been classified as "hostile Type A's" throughout their adult lives have greater problems caring for a loved one. Their anger may show in depression.

The one being cared for also picks up on this hostility and sort of "gives up," according to psychiatry professor Peter Vitaliano. His studies show that those being cared for by less hostile caregivers maintain their health longer and better.

"The thing is," Vitaliano says, "the patients we checked weren't different in mental status, but they were different in how they washed and groomed themselves. They simply didn't try as hard if they were in a hostile environment. So, we focused on the caregivers of the patients who weren't doing so well and found that they were hostile and depressed and this spilled over onto the patients. These caregivers tended to avoid problems instead of coping with them. They rarely counted their blessings.

"Then we looked at their psychological charac-teristics, and we found that fourteen of the nineteen caregivers who had been identified as hostile had previously or currently dealt with cancer or cardiovascular disease, while only sixteen out of the seventy-five who had limited hostility had suffered or were suffering from cancer or heart disease. We're not saying that being a caregiver is what caused the cancer or heart disease, but that those who are negative or hostile are more vulnerable to these diseases, and that this spills over to the patient and they too become worse. They feed on one another," says Vitaliano.

Feelings of Being Trapped

This is one of the biggest problems faced by caregivers, according to Lindgren, who adds, "But sometimes, it's a trap of their own making. Some of them are fully aware of what they are doing by isolating themselves, but they choose to do it anyway. Many of them do it out of guilt. Others don't get away for some respite care because they have become so depressed or grief stricken that they aren't thinking clearly. The job of caregiving has become all-consuming."

Support groups can help these people recognize their needs, although the research on these groups offers conflicting conclusions. Some studies indicate that when people attend support groups, it helps to forestall placement of the loved one in an institution. Other studies indicate that it doesn't offer the relief it's supposed to because it becomes nothing but a big complaint session.

Research by Vernon Greene of Syracuse University, which included well-monitored and professionally staffed support groups, showed that the caregivers attending these quality support groups were better able to cope with their caregiving responsibilities. This included taking better care of themselves.

Lindgren points out, however, that some support groups simply reinforce the hostile feelings. "They hire a sitter so they can get out to go to a support meeting, and then all they talk about is caregiving. Even when they get away, the meeting is consumed with talk of caregiving.

"What they need is time away from the role of caregiver. They need to learn some things about themselves and to do some relaxation therapy, or exercise, instead of just talking about the problem. But there is so much social guilt about taking care of yourself when the other person seems to need so much, that this isn't done."

Vitaliano says depression is common among caregivers. "Many of them tend to deny depression, but as you talk with them and as they get more comfortable, they are more open. Some feel it is their duty and that they shouldn't have these negative feelings. Others are quite open about it."

Chronic depression should be considered life-threatening. It's different from the temporary depression all of us suffer at difficult times in that it doesn't lift, may last for weeks at a time, and interferes with work and recreation. If you're experiencing severe bouts of depression, seek professional help.

Becker's studies, done chiefly with those caring for Alzheimer's patients, and mostly to analyze levels of depression in caregivers, indicate that those who don't complain about their caregiving role seem to be physically healthier than those who complain.

Surprisingly, institutionalizing the loved one doesn't reduce the level of depression in caregivers, according to Becker, because the caregiver hasn't dealt with many of the emotional issues draining their strength and resolve. The caregiver often hasn't let go of the fact that their loved one is not the same individual they once knew.

Becker's studies also indicate that depression is linked to control over the situation. If the patient's condition worsens and the caregiver is unprepared to accept or anticipate these changes, the caregiver's depression gets worse.

Those who maintain good physical health and have high self-esteem are more apt to create a positive support system for themselves and avoid becoming isolated.

Chronic Grief

"One of the main issues is chronic grief," says Lindgren. "If the one being cared for had died, the person left behind would be able to complete the grieving process and move on with their lives. But when someone is ill and is not going to recover, yet requires hours and hours of their time and there is no reciprocation, it's as if they have lost a companion but can't complete their grief."

Lindgren believes that most caregivers need counseling, even if only briefly, to help them understand what they are dealing with. "Because their lives are still bound up in this, they can't grieve," she says.

Unfortunately, counseling services can be costly and, as yet, there are no provisions in **Medicare** to pay for them. "I think eventually there will be provisions made through government or private insurance companies to provide some form of counseling to the caregivers, like in hospice programs," says Lindgren.

Hospice, which is designed for terminally ill patients, allows the caregiver to receive two grief visits from a professional after the loved one has died. Hospice care can be paid for by **Medicare**, if the patient qualifies, or through other certified programs (check with your local hospice to see what funding is available).

Life Revolves Around Caregiving Role

Many caregivers feel a deep satisfaction caring for their loved ones, especially spouses who look after their husbands or wives after many years of marriage. However, these caregivers experience the same problems of depression as other caregivers if they don't allow for respite time. And the same problems exist for sons and daughters who care for a parent who is frail or who has dementia.

Many of the studies on caring for the aged have centered on Alzheimer's patients and their caregivers, whether they be husbands, wives, daughters or sons providing the care. Caregivers of Alzheimer's patients tend to suffer more stress than others giving care because of the full-time demands made on them. It's been estimated that in a hospital setting, Alzheimer's patients require at least eleven hours of a nurses time each day. For those giving care at home without the resources the hospital has, the time can be even greater. Research shows that sixty-two percent of spouses of Alzheimer's patients experience health problems.

Bunting says that among spouses caring for Alzheimer's patients, almost all of them have no time for relaxation and about eighty percent have no relief. Children can assist caregiving parents by relieving them on occasion and encouraging them to get other forms of respite.

Often as the disease progresses, it becomes impossible to tend to Alzheimer's patients in a home environment. But even when caring for the loved one becomes dangerous, some caregivers refuse to get help.

There is still a stigma attached to getting therapy for any reason. Caregivers develop ulcers, colitis and other psychosomatic illnesses rather than availing themselves of professional help to come to terms with their grief and frustrations.

Bunting's research shows that all caregivers perform fewer self-care activities as the one being cared for demands more time and energy. Ironically, as the demands on the caregiver increase, they need more support and time to themselves in order to stay healthy, so they can provide the care.

Bunting believes that the caregiver would be ahead of the game if he or she allowed a nurse to come into the home to show them the easiest ways to care for the elderly—such as how to bathe them. This one-time visit could lessen the load of the caregiver as he or she learns easier ways to handle certain caregiving duties. All too often, however, people are reluctant to seek this outside help, to get short-term care for the parent, or to talk about their hostile feelings or grief. It is incumbent upon caregivers to recognize their own health needs and to care for themselves.

Suggested health measures are:

- Eat balanced meals.
- Maintain required sleep.
- Get respite.
- Attend support groups.
- Get counseling if necessary.
- Read materials about caregiving.
- Get exercise such as yoga or walking.
- Take the one being cared for to a day-care center.
- Learn to accept and deal with feelings such as guilt and anger.
- Get regular medical checkups.
- Ask for help whenever possible.

Not all aspects of caregiving are stressful or burden-some. Laughter and love remain part of our everyday experience and provide welcome relief. I can look back on some happy, even funny times. Some, of course, weren't so funny at the time. My dad and I were talking in the kitchen one day before his stroke about a parade he'd been in and Mom was in the living room. She began accusing us of talking about her behind her back. When we tried to reassure her that we weren't discussing her, she began shouting, "Bullshit! Bullshit!" (This was highly uncharacteristic of her.)

Rather than continue the argument, Daddy and I just shrugged our shoulders and let her continue her tirade until it was over, knowing that eventually she would forget the whole episode.

Despite the fact that my mother can't remember what she said five minutes ago, or that you visited her last week, she comes up with some Lulus.

In the hospital after her mastectomy in 1988, she looked at me seriously and said, "Rita Sue, they took off one of my breasts."

I was just about ready to burst into tears, until she added, "But I still have more than you do." I happen to be quite small.

Another time in the hospital she said, "The nurses just told me something to do and I can't remember what it was." I picked up her chart at the end of the bed and noticed there was no mention of her having Alzheimer's. I hied it down to the nurses station and asked those in attendance if they were aware of my mother's condition.

"No," they said. "No wonder she never does anything we tell her."

Which brings to mind that sometimes it's the little nitty gritty things like this that need attending, and not big, seemingly unsolvable problems.

After the surgery, Mom refused to wear the prosthesis for which she was fitted. "Weighs like a ton of sand," she said. "These socks I've been stuffing in are just as good and a lot lighter."

Daddy shrugged his shoulders and started laughing. "Whatever makes her happy," he said.

Many changes have occurred in my life recently, and when I reflect on them I become aware that they have forced me to grow emotionally and spiritually.

Keeping Your Parent Healthy & Happy 7

OUR IMAGES OF AGING have changed dramatically in the past ten years. Aging processes we once considered inevitable are now being tested and treated in order to help provide a higher quality of life as we age. Technology and new medications help us deal with many illnesses that used to herald the end of an active life. Today's life span is about seventy-five years, but it's expected to reach nearly one hundred in the next century because of increased knowledge about aging, new technologies, and the nation's move to a healthier lifestyle. This is not to say there is a fountain of youth. We are all going to wrinkle and develop conditions that slow us down, in addition to other natural aging processes. But most of us can look forward to a more healthful and longer life than our grandparents enjoyed.

Many social misconceptions about aging are falling by the wayside, as well. An example of the changes in our perception is the fact that more than half the runners who finished the 1989 Boston Marathon were over forty. Twenty years ago most of us believed that only high school and college athletes were capable of running.

Older people today have more money, more leisure and see themselves differently than did our grandparents. Additionally, the baby boomers have hit their forties, and as a group, they're not the type to sit still and take getting old lightly.

Exercise and Diet

According to the UC Berkeley Wellness Letter, exercise is one of the most important factors in having a healthy life, even in old age. "Regular exercise has been shown to inhibit, arrest, or even reverse most such declines. Some experts estimate that half the functional losses that set in between the ages of thirty and seventy can be attributed to lack of exercise." (Vol. 5, issue 9.)

For example, although diabetes caused by difficulty in metabolizing glucose is common in the aged, this glucose/carbohydrate intolerance isn't necessarily the result of biological aging. Studies suggest that improved diet and exercise habits can substantially increase glucose tolerance.

Also, inactivity can result in bone loss or osteoporosis. A lifetime of weight-bearing exercise such as walking or certain forms of weight lifting, can slow down the disease.

Maria Fiatarone, a researcher at the Veteran's Administration Medical Center in Los Angeles, California, found that exercise improves certain immune system functions in healthy older people as effectively as it does in younger people. Although the immune system appears to decline with age, and reduced physical activity from bed rest or immobilization causes added declines, exercise seems to help bring the immune system back up. "All the studies that have been done on exercise and the immune system are basically done on younger people. I looked at old people and found that exercise affects their immune systems too," she says.

Fiatarone believes it's extremely important to keep the elderly mobile. "A person who is bedridden can be rehabilitated. I think we need to change our attitudes about it. We think it's normal for the elderly to sit around. There are changes that occur in the muscles with aging but they are relatively minor." Her studies also show that when nursing home residents start weight lifting, even if they've been sedentary for twenty or thirty years, they can be rehabilitated.

"The caregiver can do exercise with the parent— walking with them, or whatever," Fiatarone says. "Even simple kinds of functions which strengthen muscles will lessen some of the dependence on a caregiver. There's a lot that can be done in the home without going to a gym." If the caregiver is confined to the home with the elderly parent, Fiatarone suggests the use of ankle weights while sitting in a chair, stairways and stationary bicycles. Before beginning an exercise routine with an elderly parent in the home, the caregiver should check with a physician or a home therapist.

Other ways to boost the health of your parent include: limiting alcohol and caffeine consumption, not smoking, and eating fruits, vegetables, proteins and grains, while reducing the amounts of saturated fats in the diet.

We can encourage our parents to make healthful changes in their lifestyles, but we should bear in mind that this is not the only way we can help them. Understanding, love and patience go a long way to add enjoyment to your parents' later years and are usually more effective than judgmental criticism in helping them change their lifestyles.

For example, if your mother or father has become inactive, you might try walking with them, rather than just suggesting that they get some exercise. If they smoke and you consider it dangerous for reasons other than their general well-being, such as a safety hazard in the house, establish conditions for smoking as we did with my mother. We put her cigarettes where she couldn't reach them and explained that she would have to ask us for one, and then she could smoke it only if someone were available to sit with her while she smoked.

In making these suggestions to parents, it's a personal belief of mine that we don't have the right as their adult children to look askance at them for habits that we now consider unhealthful. Much of the information on cholesterol, smoking and exercise that has come to our attention in the past few years, was unknown to them when they were developing their patterns of living.

These new health findings always make headlines. Smaller news stories are written when these findings are challenged by other research. As an example, we've been lead to believe that adding water and roughage to the diets of older people will prevent constipation, a common problem. New research, however, indicates that it may not lessen the problem of constipation at all. Constipation may be the result of a loss of certain cells in the large intestine, which is a normal part of aging. These cells determine water content in the stools, and without this function constipation occurs, says Mark Donowitz, M.D., chief of gastroenterology at Johns Hopkins. So, certain types of medication may be necessary, rather than adding more fiber and water to the diet.

Medication

But medication is another arena where caregivers must stay on the ball. It's a good policy to keep track of the medications our loved one is taking and to find out how a new prescription may affect them.

Bradley Williams, professor of clinical pharmacy and gerontology, believes families who are providing care for a parent have a right to ask the parent's physician to have a pharmacist, preferably a gerontological pharmacist, look at the drug regimen.

A trained pharmacist is aware of how various drugs interact and how they affect specific individuals at different ages.

It is not unusual for elderly people with numerous health problems, especially those who are hospitalized, to be taking a vast array of medications prescribed by a variety of physicians. A reduction in the amount of medication being given is usually desirable, and detection of potentially dangerous combinations of drugs can be lifesaving.

Williams was part of a pilot program at Rancho Los Amigo Medical Center in Downey, California, that reduced some medications being given patients by up to fifty percent through the use of "pharmaceutical rounds" at the hospital. These rounds involved having a specially trained pharmacist assess the medicinal regimens of each patient. In one extreme case, a seventy-three-year-old diabetic woman who was taking twenty-one different medications when she entered the hospital, left taking two routine medications and three as-needed prescriptions, according to Williams.

Unfortunately, most hospitals do not provide these pharmaceutical rounds. But reduction and productive changes in medication needn't take place at the hospital. Home-health-care managers, or care coordinators, responsible for post-hospital care can accomplish the task with the addition of a pharmacist to the health care team. Carefully planned drug treatment makes it easier for caregivers to manage a patient in the home. Additionally, it gives the caregiver and the patient more confidence in their ability to manage the medication, which, in itself, provides a sense of well-being.

"Many changes occur with the physiology of people. As they age, they become less able to handle medications. The medications are eliminated from the body more slowly, and older people are more susceptible to adverse effects, particularly prescriptions that affect the brain. The risks simply become higher," Williams says.

Adding to the problems associated with prescription drugs and the elderly is the fact that most drug testing has been done on younger people, gerontologist Richard Lindsay, M.D., says.

Williams points out that, "Physicians are trained to place primary importance on diagnosis and overall treatment. They cannot be expected to be experts in clinical pharmacology, pharmacokinetics (the body's absorption, distribution, metabolism and elimination of a drug), and pharmacodynamics (a drug's interaction at its site of activity in the body)."

But Lindsay believes that physicians should be acquainted with the special drug needs of the elderly, and that geriatric material needs to be taught in the nation's medical schools. "It's also imperative that the caregiver as well as the patient understand the side effects of any given drug and watch for signs of change that could be related to drugs. That way, I'm doubling my chances that if any adverse reactions occur, I'll be notified," he says. Symptoms of negative drug reactions in the elderly include: weakness and lethargy or tiredness; a rash; confusion that didn't exist before the drug was administered; depression; altered excretions; muscle contractions; and trouble with speech.

Lindsay recommends that all old medications should be thrown out. "It sometimes seems foolish to throw them away. You think there might be an eventual use for them, but taking some drugs when they're old can cause problems. A drug like tetracycline, if it's old, can damage the kidneys. Just take them out of the medicine cabinet and toss them away," he says.

Another problem is with over-the-counter drugs. "People think they don't have to worry about them, but they should. Some cold remedies have anticholinergic properties, and if taken with prescribed drugs that also have anticholinergic properties, it may overload the system and cause pressure in the eyes (more trouble if the person has glaucoma), or if they have prostrate trouble, it might cause urinary retention," he says. So, always tell your physician about any over-the-counter drugs your parent commonly uses.

Aging Processes

Unfortunately, some inevitable health problems that we experience as we age can't be deterred by improving lifestyle or reducing a drug regimen. But an awareness of aging processes will help us understand the behavior of our parents and, eventually, ourselves when we are elderly.

It's been said that once we're born, we begin preparing for death. That's debatable, but certainly by the time we're in our late teens, we are beginning to deteriorate. We do so at our own rates. We all know people in their fifties with unlined faces and others who have not one gray hair. Much of this is determined through heredity.

But all of us, by middle age or a little later, have narrowed blood vessels that slow down our circulation. We lose muscle fiber, and the speed at which messages travel from brain to nerve endings decreases. Many of us begin experiencing chronic illness such as arthritis, hypertension and diabetes. These simply become a part of our lives, but not a cause to stop living normally. We learn to take care, rather than to look for a cure. The rate at which these things happen depends a great deal on our own particular lifestyles.

Still, we can count on our skin beginning to dry out because our sweat and sebaceous glands function less effectively. We may bruise more easily. We may think our mother or father has had a really bad fall or accident because of the bruises or breaks in the skin on their arm, when, in fact, it doesn't take much to injure the skin of an elderly person.

And, most of us at one time or another have walked into an older person's home and wondered why they have the heat up so high when we seem to be suffocating. Because of their age and blood circulation, they simply feel the cold more readily.

Many elderly suffer from incontinence and it is often dismissed as part of growing old. The family may not even be aware that the parent is suffering from poor bladder control until the parent is placed in a nursing home or hospital. It's been estimated that nearly half of women over the age of fifty have varying degrees of poor bladder control and accidents. It's a hidden problem because it's misunderstood.

The causes of incontinence include reduction in bladder capacity; difficulty in getting to the bathroom on time because of other medical problems; medications such as tranquilizers, diuretics or intravenous feeding; bladder or urinary tract infections; damage to the sphincter (the muscle controlling contraction or release of the bladder); and problems with dementia, stroke or severe bodily injuries. Incontinence naturally frustrates a caregiver and often leads to placement of the elderly person in a nursing facility. But in some cases, it's treatable and correctable, and the elderly should be encouraged to have the problem checked by a physician.

Many problems that the elderly are plagued by stem from the diminishing of the five senses—smell, taste, hearing, sight and touch. As many of us have experienced, when we don't have full use of one of our senses, we feel disoriented and often must withdraw from certain activities.

Losing an acute sense of smell can jeopardize our physical and mental health. Our ability to avoid life-threatening situations such as escaping gas or smoke from a fire, is greatly reduced. Also, a diminished sense of smell depletes our enjoyment of good food because the sense of taste is dependent on our ability to smell. The lack of taste causes some to turn aside from wholesome foods that seem lackluster in comparison to some junk foods. Medical psychologist Susan Schiffman says that many elderly people who lose their appetites fail to eat nourishing food and become more incapacitated than they need be. This can be helped with flavor enhancers that make the food more appealing.

"Spicy foods don't usually appeal to the elderly, but flavor enhancers such as low-sodium bacon bits, and liquid flavors such as vanilla, banana, rum, maple, strawberry and chocolate can be used on certain foods," she says. "What these flavorings do is add more molecules for the person to smell and they will like the food better."

Since food plays an important role in our social lives, people with smell problems frequently avoid social contact, which, in turn, can lead to depression. Robert Henkin, M.D., of the Taste & Smell Center in Washington D.C., says, "People with smell problems come to me depressed. They don't know what to do. They go to their family physician and the doctor tells them to go home and learn to live with it. It's a hidden handicap. If someone is blind or has a broken leg, they're treated for it, but losing the sense of smell doesn't appear to be life threatening, so it's ignored."

If your parent is having smell problems, review the side effects of any medication they're taking with their physician because some drug therapies can affect the sense of smell.

Hearing loss, though normal with aging, is aggravated by our noisy culture. Noise has been identified worldwide as a major health problem and many industrialized countries have initiated laws to protect people against noise bombardment.

Hearing loss affects people in two ways: "People with conductive hearing loss, in which sound doesn't reach the inner ear because of problems with the sound organs (such as the eardrum), hear themselves clearly, but can't hear others," says hearing specialist, Wiley Harrison, M.D. The other type of hearing loss is sensorineural hearing, involving problems of the inner ear, which forces a person to speak more loudly in order to hear him or herself.

Our sight begins to decrease in our early twenties. Our eyes adapt to changes in light and dark more slowly, we lose some peripheral vision and, just as our skin loses its elasticity, so does the eye lens, which also reduces our visual field.

Add a diminishing loss of the sense of touch, slower reflexes, and loss of teeth, and we may begin to understand not only our parents' altered physical appearance and urge to stay close to home, but also some of the psychological changes they are undergoing as they experience these physical changes.

Alzheimer's Disease

Alzheimer's disease is often referred to as the "silent epidemic," or "the disease of the century," afflicting up to four million Americans. It is a degenerative disease of the central nervous system that attacks the brain and results in impaired memory, thinking and behavior. More than 100,000 die of Alzheimer's disease annually making it the fourth leading cause of death in adults after heart disease, cancer and stroke.

Most Alzheimer's victims are over sixty-five, and it's estimated that half of those over eighty-five, which is the fastest growing segment of the population, will suffer from Alzheimer's by the year 2000. It can also strike people in their forties and fifties, as it did Rita Hayworth. However, only about five percent of people over sixty-five have severe memory loss because of Alzheimer's and ten percent have mild loss.

Alzheimer's is not the same as dementia or some of the other one hundred disorders that can mimic the same symptoms. Unlike Alzheimer's, most of these other disorders can be treated, reversed and some can be cured. Alzheimer's is one of the most debilitating and costly to treat of the afflictions that beset the aged. As an example, it's estimated that treating Alzheimer's patients in this country costs upwards of $80 billion annually. Also, Alzheimer's patients make up half of those in nursing homes. By the year 2050, fourteen million elderly may be suffering the ravages of the disease according to a recent Newsweek article.

Depression and Suicide

Your elderly parent may become depressed for a number of understandable reasons. They are losing friends and close relatives to death. Their safe worlds are being uprooted. They are losing independence, especially if they move in with the caregiver. If they are on high levels of medication, they may feel disoriented and out of control.

Research at Stanford University indicates that when the elderly move from another part of the country to be near their grown sons and daughters, they usually suffer depression brought about by leaving friends and familiar surroundings. Researcher Pat Henley-Peterson says a move is the number one cause of depression in the people they see at the university's geriatric center.

After my mom was admitted to a psychiatric ward, they began treating her depression. Even though she is far into her dementia with Alzheimer's, she's aware in lucid moments that she has it and this depresses her. She's depressed because she can't care for her husband and she's depressed because of all the changes made in her home—her home that she has been in charge of for years.

The good news is that depression in older people is as treatable as it is in younger persons. Some studies indicate that the elderly respond faster to treatment than younger people do. Robert Knight, author of *Outreach with the Elderly: Community Education, Assessment and Therapy*, says that his studies clearly show that older adults benefit from therapy. Knight and many other gerontologists believe that when older people are carefully assessed and screened, behavior assumed to be the result of physical problems may instead be a symptom of a mental disorder.

About twenty percent of people over the age of sixty-five suffer from depression. Experts believe that depression is the leading cause of suicide among the elderly. And, older Americans have a suicide rate that is fifty percent higher than that of the general population, according to a report by the American Association of Retired Person's Public Policy Institute.

It's unfortunate that my mother didn't begin receiving treatment for her depression until she had attempted suicide, but she's one of the lucky ones in that she did not succeed. Research indicates that an older person is more likely to succeed at a suicide attempt than a younger person. They usually use more violent means, such as guns or razor blades, rather than pills.

Household Safety

In addition to looking after a parent's physical and psychological well-being, simple changes can be made in the home to make it safer and more accommodating. "There are low-cost physical changes that can be made in the home to make life easier for both the caregiver and the elderly person," says Jon Pynoos, one of the authors of "Home Evaluation Resource Booklet for the Elderly." (See "Resources" for information on how to obtain this booklet.) Such items as hand-held showers and sticky tape to put on the bottom of bathtubs make life easier and safer in a caregiving household.

Some of the other tips Pynoos offers are:

- Use cloth or foam on a doorknob, secured with a rubber band for easier turning.
- Install lights above or near doors.
- Put colored tape on keys for a better grasp.

- Install louder doorbells.
- Put covering on stairs that will prevent slipping.
- Use pegboards to hang frequently used items.
- Lower the setting on the hot water heater to 120 degrees to reduce risk of scalding.
- Keep a flashlight by the bed.
- Secure any throw rugs to the floor to prevent slipping.
- Use a large telephone template to make visibility easier.
- List emergency numbers plus those of physicians and close friends near the phone in large print.

Pynoos advises against making the home look like an institution, emphasizing that it's important for the home to remain familiar and comfortable.

There are obstacles. It isn't always easy to get in touch with the loved one's physician. They may not like suggestions such as getting the opinion of a gerontological pharmacist. Funding agencies may balk at your requests for certain supplies. It may take time to achieve your goals, but in the long run, taking charge of the situation will save time and make life easier and safer for you and your loved one.

Who Pays 8

MANY ELDERLY PEOPLE AND THEIR FAMILIES believe that the social security administration's Medicare insurance program provides coverage for all medical needs. These people are in for a rude awakening when they discover that Medicare provides next to nothing for long-term care.

As an advocate for your parents, you will need a working knowledge of the following types of health care coverage in order to discern where the money for their care will come from:

MEDICARE is the federal health insurance program for people over the age of sixty-five. It doesn't cover long-term care unless the patient is first hospitalized and then placed in a nursing home to be rehabilitated, or treated at home by skilled-nursing care. Even then there may be limitations. In my father's case, Medicare had provisions to pay for his care following his stroke for up to 150 days. They ended up cutting his allowable days even further though, because he belonged to a Health Maintenance Organization (HMO). Acute care is well covered by Medicare. Long-term care isn't.

MEDICAID (Medi-Cal in California) pays for more than half of all long-term care patients. It is a federal program administered by individual states. The administering agency varies in every state. In California, it is administered through the Department of Public Social Services, under the jurisdiction of the State Department of Social Services, which operates from the state's Health and Welfare Department. In other states, it may fall under the jurisdiction of the health department or the department of welfare. Your physician or your state's unit on aging will be able to give you the proper name of the agency to contact.

In order to qualify for Medicaid, a person can only own a certain amount of property and have limited amounts of liquid assets. Income splitting, which involves dividing the income of a couple, can make one eligible for public assistance such as Medicaid.

As an example, before my father died, his eligibility was determined by splitting their net worth in half. My mother's eligibility was also determined by half of their net worth. Once my father died, the entire estate went to Mother and it changed her status. Since she is sole owner of the property now, Medicaid can take a portion of the money from the sale of the house to pay certain costs of her care unless it is determined by the courts that the living trust my parents had drawn up a few years ago protects that property from confiscation.

MEDICARE SUPPLEMENTAL INSURANCE (Medigap), a type of insurance that can be purchased through several independent companies, usually pays for certain costs not covered by Medicare. It doesn't help in most long-term care situations.

VETERANS BENEFITS. Depending on eligibility requirements that fluctuate, the Veterans Administration accepts some, but not all long-term care patients. They also accept some, but not all military dependents requiring long-term care.

SOCIAL SECURITY DISABILITY (SSD). This program assists in long-term care for those workers who have paid into the fund and are eligible. SSD is an aid to disabled workers whose impairments prohibit them from returning to work.

SUPPLEMENTAL SECURITY INCOME (SSI). This program is similar to SSD, but is based on the income level of disabled persons in addition to the limits placed on them by their disability.

PRIVATE INSURANCE. Until recently, private insurance companies have turned their back on long-term care, but some are now offering limited insurance for nursing home care and they are taking a look at some of the new, innovative programs, such as in-home care, and programs designed to assist the elderly to live in their own homes as long as possible with specialized services. But these new insurance plans are separate from regular medical policies and many can be quite expensive.

You should be extremely careful when purchasing private insurance for long-term care protection. The costs, limitations and restrictions should be carefully scrutinized before purchasing such policies. Dr. James Firman, president of the United Seniors Health Cooperative, writes in a report, "The average probability that a private insurance policy holder would not collect any benefits after entering a nursing home was sixty-one percent; only eighteen percent of the policies studied offering long-term care provided better than a fifty-fifty chance of ever paying benefits. Many of the policies now being offered for sale are contrary to both consumer and public interests because they are not likely to pay adequate benefits if and when people use them." Private insurance currently pays for less than five percent of all long-term care patients.

HEALTH MAINTENANCE ORGANIZA-TIONS (HMOs) are prepaid health care organizations that limit what hospitals and physicians an enrollee can use. An HMO can be used in combination with Medicare to meet expenses not covered by Medicare. The HMO takes all of the patient's Medicare and provides medical coverage without additional cost. If the patient goes on Medicaid, the HMO can continue handling their coverage.

PREFERRED PROVIDER ORGANIZATIONS (PPOs), like HMOs, also set limits on the physicians an enrollee can use. Patients have their choice of physicians from a list of names provided by the PPOs. Both PPOs and HMOs make an effort to cut costs by strict quality control.

Other sources that can be tapped for help in caring for your parent are the Older Americans Act and Social Services Block Grants that provide funds for such services as home delivered meals, case management, chore services such as yard work, adult day care, senior centers, transportation, and companion services.

Additionally, some states have what is called a "reverse annuity mortgage long-term care loan program." This plan allows an elderly person to remain in their own home by obtaining loans on the house to pay for health care costs. This type of loan can also be used to help pay nursing home expenses.

Paying for long-term care requires many sources of financial aid and none are as readily available as we'd like them to be. Tapping into some of these sources and protecting the assets of your parent, or yourself, sometimes takes the expertise of an attorney.

When I contacted the Inland Counties Resource Center for brain-impaired adults, I was given the names of several attorneys that specialize in helping families obtain eligibility for Medi-Cal. This particular resource center is one of several mandated by the state of California, but not all states have such centers.

Figuring out what type of coverage your parents need and how to apply for it takes time. Following my father's stroke, when it became evident that we would have to handle my parents' financial affairs, we felt fortunate that they had placed our names on their checking account. We were able to immediately set up a special account especially to handle their finances and to show accountability of what we were doing with that money. It was a small amount—$3,000—and within the first three weeks of his stroke, nearly $2,000 of it had been used up paying their bills, getting supplies for Dad when he came home from the nursing home, and buying food and other supplies for the in-home caregiver. We also had to pay for prescriptions for Mom and Dad, because we hadn't yet received Medi-Cal stickers and didn't know of the other sources we could tap for financial assistance.

Even if your parents have good medical insurance and plenty of savings, they may be forced to spend their savings on in-home care simply to become eligible for Medicaid. Prior to September 1989, in some states, after the death of a spouse who had been receiving Medicaid, the state was allowed to confiscate the survivor's home to help offset the expenses picked up by the state's Medicaid program.

One social worker told me about an elderly man and his wife who, two years ago, were seeking Medicaid for the husband and were asked to sign over their house on the spot when applying for assistance through their state agency. This action, and others like it, is illegal, but until recently, no one had challenged the state agencies on this matter.

Couples are now protected by new laws adopted first in California, and then in the nation, because of the work of one man—Marc Hankin, an attorney whose mother was no longer able to care for his father who had

Alzheimer's. Hankin, now a Los Angeles elder-law attorney with the firm of Fulbright and Jaworski, recalls that his journey as a caregiver's advocate, which began in the early 1980s, was spurred by the fear of his mother becoming a bag lady.

His mother called him in New York, where he was pursuing a post-jurus doctoral program in tax law. He had just been hired as a clerk for a former chief justice of the Supreme Court. When his mother told him she could no longer handle his dad's Alzheimer's, he returned home and helped her take care of his father for a couple of years. He finally had to place his father in a veteran's hospital when they could no longer handle the situation.

He had worked on conservatorship papers for his mother and then began doing it for others. "Then, I realized that conservatorships were only part of the solution that enabled you to place somebody in a nursing facility, but it still left the surviving spouse with the threat of being wiped out financially," he says.

Following a hassle from Medi-Cal officials when he asked for a copy of its regulations, Hankin began researching Medi-Cal law. He concluded that under the existing laws, his parents' home could be gifted to his mother and wouldn't interfere with his father's Medi-Cal. Also, the remaining assets could be divided equally—half to his mother and half to his father—so that when his father used up his half he would be eligible for Medi-Cal in a nursing home and his mom would be able to keep the home and her half of the assets.

Hankin proposed his idea to the health services system, pointing out that existing statutes clearly allowed for this method of "asset and income splitting," and recommending that the state make this option known to those applying for Medi-Cal. After speaking with many officials, he finally found himself face-to-face with the department's top eligibility law expert. The law expert for health services wouldn't budge, although he agreed with Hankin's findings. "Our policy is that they have to spend everything before we can help with Medi-Cal," Hankin recalls the expert saying.

Hankin's efforts came to a standstill until September 1982, when the Assembly Committee on Long-Term Care held a public hearing on Alzheimer's in San Diego. Hankin literally begged a spot to testify and put together a brief that eventually laid the groundwork for the laws passed in 1985 protecting the assets of surviving spouses. During this period, Hankin lived close to the poverty level himself, but says it was all worth it. "It was a once in a lifetime chance to do something really good that I would feel great about all my life."

Of the California law, and later federal laws that saved millions of surviving spouses from poverty, Hankin says, "Remember that my statute only clarified existing laws. Even the lawyers didn't know the people's rights." Hankin says that in his law practice he deals with some very complicated issues, but that nothing is more complicated than our health care laws and how they affect the elderly.

The California bill laid the groundwork for the portions of the 1988 Medicare Catastrophic Coverage

Act that protect surviving spouses. The act stipulates that states must allow the spouse of the person receiving Medicaid to retain at least $786 per month from income and other assets and a minimal amount of liquid assets or resources, in addition to the couple's home. Check with the agency handling your parent's Medicaid application for exact figures. Although portions of the act have since been eliminated or watered down under recent moves to repeal the law, most of the spousal property protection provisions were preserved.

If you think this is beginning to sound complicated, it is nothing compared to what you will have to face if your parents become unable to administer their own financial and legal affairs. You should familiarize yourself with the importance of the following documents, and have the necessary ones drawn up *before* your aging parents become seriously ill. It is equally important that you and your whole family fill out these forms for yourselves, to be covered in the event of an accident.

DURABLE POWER OF ATTORNEY FOR HEALTH CARE. This document designates a specific person the "agent" to make health care decisions for you if you are unconscious or otherwise incapable of giving "informed consent." It also allows you to stipulate whether or not you want life-sustaining treatment in various situations. The document must be in accordance with your state's civil codes. California residents can obtain a durable power of attorney for health care form from the California Medical Association, P.O. Box 7690, San Francisco, CA 94120.

THE LIVING WILL. This document, sometimes known as a "directive to physicians," specifically requests that you not be kept alive by artificial means or "heroic measures." Unfortunately, some states do not fully recognize the legality of this document. The durable power of attorney for health care provides stronger legal protection for the doctors who are treating you.

CONSERVATORSHIP. A designated person or persons, usually a family member, is designated the guardian or protector of the person's health care, finances or both. The designated guardian is accountable to the courts for their actions involving the estate. Establishing conservatorship is a very involved process and usually requires at least one court appearance. For example, in order for my sister and I to establish conservatorship for my mother, testimony of her incompetence is required from other relatives and they have the right to contest our petition for conservatorship.

CERTIFICATION OF MENTAL INCOMPE-TENCE. This document is required before a conservatorship can become effective. The procedure varies in different states, but usually requires the signatures of more than one physician, and can be contested by other relatives, and in some cases, by the person for whom the certification is being sought.

DURABLE POWER OF ATTORNEY. It's similar to a durable power of attorney for health care, but it also allows an individual to tend to the person's financial, as well as health matters. It is done with the person's consent and must be established *before* the person is deemed incapable of making decisions.

INTERSPOUSAL AGREEMENT. This document used to be helpful in preventing spousal impoverishment but Los Angeles attorney Marc Hankin says that couples attempting to avoid spousal impoverishment should not rely on Interspousal Agreements. Instead, they should obtain special court orders, authorized by the Medicare Catastrophic Coverage Act, specifically protecting various assets. Those assets should be placed in special trusts designed to comply with those court orders.

LIVING TRUST. More people than ever before are obtaining revocable living trusts to protect their assets and save other family members the headache and heartache of going through probate, which in some states can tie up assets for years. With a living trust, property, securities and other assets are placed in a trust while the owner is still alive. Instructions within the trust, which are drawn up by an attorney, serve as guidelines for managing and distributing the assets after the individual's death. The individual making the trust can change it at any time. Attorney's fees for establishing the trust range from about $800 to $2,000.

If a living trust is drawn up correctly, it can also establish conservatorships or durable powers of attorney that will save adult children countless hours of work when the parents become incapacitated.

We were fortunate in that when Mom was diagnosed with Alzheimer's we had encouraged Daddy to have a living trust drawn up so that we would be protected in the event of his or her death. Even with this trust, we have had to employ the services of a lawyer in order to obtain conservatorship for my mother, because letters from physicians declaring her incompetent must be worded in accordance with certain provisions of the trust.

The reason my sister and I needed the power to sign legal documents for my parents was because my father's signature after his stroke wasn't legal because he couldn't write his name. He did make an "X" a couple of times with witnesses present so that we could obtain certain information, such as his veteran's status. Mother's signature, until the conservatorship is in place, is still legal in some instances, such as obtaining her signature in order to get a final bank statement from an account that had been closed. We need such a statement as proof that no money exists in the account or her Medi-Cal status will be denied.

If you're fortunate, your parents will have already provided some type of will, a living trust, or are still capable of assigning you power of attorney. These documents not only protect the assets for a surviving spouse, or the children, but provide an instrument whereby a terminally ill, comatose or brain-impaired patient can make his or her wishes known regarding life-support systems and burial procedures.

However, various surveys indicate that only about five percent of those over sixty-five make it known in a living will or durable power of attorney whether or not they even want to be placed on life-support systems. In the case of my father, he did not, unfortunately, make a provision in his living trust for the use or non-use of extraordinary measures, so we had to fill out special papers stating no extraordinary measures. Few people have the foresight to take care of such matters before it is too late and, thus, the issues become even more complicated.

Researchers at the Geriatrics Section and Center for Clinical Medical Ethics at the University of Chicago are studying why the elderly don't empower themselves by making their wishes known. Patricia Jo Wilkinson, an attorney specializing in living trusts, says that many people don't want to think about wills and trusts until they become ill. "By that time it's usually too late," she says.

Once we began tapping into Medi-Cal, and once Mom had been admitted to a psychiatric ward, we knew the legal and financial issues were getting too complicated for us to handle, partly because we had become so emotionally drained. At this point, we obtained professional legal help. Even if your parents' situation is not that complicated, it can be a welcome relief to have someone else handling the paperwork for you. Names of attorneys specializing in legal matters concerning the elderly and their children, such as for guardianships, living trusts, wills, and who can be of service getting families into the "system," can be obtained through state bar associations, friends who have used such services, and organizations that serve the needs of the elderly, such as the Inland Counties Resource Center.

Laws concerning guardianships, conservatorships, power of attorney, trusts, wills, and interspousal agreements vary from state to state and are subject to change. So, it is wise to contact an attorney, especially if no legal papers have been drawn up by your parents. Even if they have, you may reach a point where you need the advice of a lawyer, especially if you are dealing with an Alzheimer's patient.

To date, age-related diseases such as Alzheimer's, which is considered a chronic condition, have been devoid of Medicare coverage. Appeals can be made to make Alzheimer's patients eligible, but only under certain conditions. Since most Alzheimer's patients don't usually require hospitalization and skilled-nursing care, it is difficult to obtain coverage even though they desperately need custodial care. Medicaid, private insurance companies, the veterans administration and some programs under social security disability can cover the costs of caring for an Alzheimer's patient, but again, only under rigid qualifications.

Ironically, and sadly, it took my mother's suicide attempt and subsequent stay in a psychiatric hospital with a psychiatrist in attendance for us to get into the system more rapidly because she now meets the requirements. Because my father's stroke required hospitalization, convalescent care and certain types of therapy afterwards, it was much easier to tap into the system for his care, as well.

Still, we had to request a hearing for Medi-Cal assistance because we were dealing with more than one agency that handles Medi-Cal qualifications: In-Home Supportive Services (which ultimately turned us down), and Medi-Cal itself, which handles medical needs. We now have a "share cost" to pay my mother's nursing facility which involves sending the nursing facility money from Mother's Social Security, as well as the Medi-Cal funds which are paid directly to the nursing facility.

Although Congress is struggling still with a repeal or a winnowing down of the 1988 Medicare Catastrophic Coverage Act, many portions are expected to remain, including laws that protect the surviving spouse's assets. Some believe that repeal of the act is a death knell to any further improvements in Medicare coverage, but others believe the fight is just beginning, especially with the impact of the babyboomers who are concerned about how they are going to care for their aging parents.

For example, Hankin is currently working at the federal level on a day-care statute, in which Medicare will pick up the tab for adult day care so that people can get relief from the stress of full-time care of an elderly family member.

To find out more about getting financial and legal aid for your parents, contact your local area agency on aging (which goes by many different names in different counties). If you can't find their number, contact the agency in your state that administers the Older American's Act (listed in the back of this book under "State Units on Aging").

❤   ❤   ❤

Because the elderly are living longer, the system of care is so complicated and families are so busy, it makes good sense to urge your parents to make some plans for their future care that will protect you and make your lives easier. Likewise, regardless of your age, you'll be ahead of the game if you get your own affairs in order so that your own family will be protected.

Americans have an abhorrence of death. We don't like to think or talk about it, although it's a natural part of life. It's something we'll have to overcome, if we are to protect our families as we would like to be protected, when we are put in the position of caring for our aging parents.

The Future of *9*
Caregiving

THE AGING OF THE POPULATION is the most powerful trend affecting the future of the health care industry, and it's impacting the lives of Americans as never before. Today, there are thirty-three million Americans drawing upon an elder care system geared to serve half that number. By the year 2,000, which is just around the corner, sixty-six million people over the age of sixty-five will bring public, private and governmental agencies to their knees unless the agencies begin changing. These agencies must face up to and find solutions to an inadequate health care system, but until then, the problems we now face in caring for the elderly will intensify for about the next ten years.

It's estimated that caring for Alzheimer's patients alone in the country today costs $39 billion annually. By the year 2030, when twenty-two percent of the population will be sixty-five or older, those costs could top $750 billion. Small wonder that government, private insurance companies, physicians and other professional groups are alarmed about long-term care.

"The demographic imperative is clear," according to a press release from Merck, Sharp & Dohme Research Laboratories. "There are more Americans over sixty-five than under twenty-five for the first time in history and the average age is steadily increasing. People over sixty-five now represent about twelve percent of the American population and utilize about thirty percent of all health care resources; these figures are projected to reach over twenty percent and fifty percent, respectively, by 2030. It is also clear that the practice of geriatrics is becoming increasingly specialized. Interest within the medical community is evidenced by the popularity of the examination, first offered in 1988, leading to a certificate of special competence in geriatrics."

The good news is, if present trends continue, we'll have an older, wiser, healthier population of the elderly. This aging, health-smart population will demand better, easier-to-access systems of elder care management—something they are already starting to do as they step into the role of caregivers for their parents.

The bad news is, caregivers of today are going to continue, for some time, to have a tough time accessing the cumbersome health care system for their parents. Hopefully, by the year 2000, they will have wrestled the government and other social agencies to the ground. It's a good bet that they will—hordes of babyboomers have been known to get what they want.

"The political reality is that the babyboomers will control the political agenda for the next twenty years. They are the largest single group of people we have," says Russell Coile, author of *The New Hospital* and *The New Medicine* and one of the first working futurists hired by a large corporation. He adds that concern for the future of caregiving is becoming more evident in some government agencies, long-term care facilities, social agencies, hospitals, home-health agencies and, increasingly, in insurance companies, HMOs and other kinds of managed health care plans.

Family caregivers save the economy about $10 billion annually. So keeping them healthy should be a priority because when they start crumbling, the one being cared for must enter the system in more costly settings, such as placement in a nursing facility.

Also, when the caregiver's health fails, the companies they work for pay. Workers caring for elderly relatives can cost a small company upwards of $200,000 per year, according to a conference sponsored by the Connecticut Community Care, Inc.

Therefore, Coile says, "Employers are starting to look at the problem, too. By the first decade of the year 2000, they will have more retirees than employees. General Motors will hit that stage by the year 2006." When they go past a one-employee-to-one-retiree ratio they will, at that point, have refashioned the factory of the future with robots and other technological innovations to take the place of fewer workers, but they will still be dealing with their retirees for a longer period of time than some of their workers, Coile says.

Burke Stinson, an AT&T headquarter's district manager, says his company's move to offer counseling services for caregivers and leaves of absences of up to a year with guarantee of their old job, is the wave of the future. AT&T is also starting a $5 million fund to establish child- and elder-care facilities near the locations of its offices and plants. "The entire package was driven by a recognition that people have a life both before they come to the office and after they leave the office. It's something corporate America should finally face up to," says Stinson. "There is no need for further studies to tell you that if you are preoccupied when you leave home or when you get home that evening, it's going to distract you while at work."

Stinson predicts that in the 1990s, elder care will become more of an issue than child care since everyone has parents, but not all have children. Companies will be very competitive because of the coming labor shortage and progressive companies that offer elder-care programs will have their choice of employees. "In the 1990s, the well-educated, talented people are going to be fewer and farther between than in the seventies and eighties, and they will be picking and choosing companies with a full range of benefits. People are concerned with something beyond their careers," says Stinson. Coile says one of the most promising trends in solving the growing problems of providing for the aged is case management. "We already have some of it but on the whole, it's fragmented. There is no central coordinating body or authority. There are no rules to govern case management. This doesn't mean we need a bunch of rules and regulations, but we don't have *any* guidelines now. Every case management organization is making up their own procedures. Each has a notion of what it means to assist an elderly person to lead an independent and quality life."

Soon, agencies will decide on a uniform set of guidelines for case management, but this doesn't help those of us who need the services now. There are still many people in nursing homes who don't really belong there because case management hasn't yet caught on. "And it's too bad because the elderly don't want to be in those places. They want to be in their own homes. They don't even want to be living with their children. They want to be at home and it's possible with managed care," Coile says.

Meanwhile, we must, by trial and error, find our way through the system. In the process, we are paving the way for the standards of future care for the elderly.

But, by the twenty-first century, all the existing demands and more will become law, Coile predicts. By the time the demands of the elderly concerning catastrophic or long-term care have been met, case management will be routine. "Providers will come out of the woodwork in response to the money that can be made from proper management of the needs of the elderly," he says. Coile sees a combination of public and private sector managers opting for case management as a way to provide quality care for the elderly. "Ideally, not only will we manage the chronically ill, but we will have a case management system in process that recognizes that life is an ongoing learning experience with a goal of optimum health and independence. Each elderly person will get an assessment of their health in regards to their daily living. In that way, we will have a personal health plan for every individual," Coile says.

Another trend that Coile foresees that will help meet the needs of elderly care is genetic probes. "Through the use of genetic probes we will have the capacity to predict, with a growing level of precision, who's going to get chronic diseases and when. Then we'll be able to plan adequate care for them before a crisis occurs.

"So much of what we do now is a knee-jerk reaction to the normal aging process. By being able to predict disease progression, we will have enough forewarning so that patients, family and caregivers can anticipate what will be needed, and what changes in lifestyle can make each individual as healthy and as independent as possible under the circumstances. While we can't prevent death, we certainly can have an impact on its premature causes. We can enhance the quality of life," Coile says.

"Ten years from now it will be the norm to help care for your aging parents, but you won't have to give up your life or your job in order to do it," he says. The help will be there, including technology that will do everything from monitoring drug dosage, to EKG's that automatically monitor heart patients three times a day. "These devices are like electronic nags. They remind a patient at regular intervals to take their drugs."

These monitoring devices are involuntary. They can trigger warning devices miles away at a health plan center or physician's office. They are an improvement over the lifeline buttons worn around the necks of heart patients, which have to be pushed in order to get help, and those are an improvement over stumbling to the telephone before passing out.

Coile's optimism is marred only by a slight stumbling block on the path to this geriatric utopia. "The problems of caring for the elderly are tame compared to what lies ahead." The turmoil and confusion we are experiencing now is going to peak before the crisis settles down. We are in what the social scientists call, "the period of awareness." We know the system needs righting because we're in pain. But that pain will give us the political clout to get things moving.

When I interviewed Steve McConnell, chairman of the Long-Term Care Campaign which is an umbrella organization dedicated to finding solutions to the problem of long-term care, I wasn't yet fully aware of the importance of his words: "We try to give people a voice and try to make sure our elected officials hear what is going on. It's very important that people have an avenue to express their frustrations and concerns. So, our campaign offers a means to express their frustrations —through advocacy. The most effective advocates are the ones on the front lines providing the care and who see things from day-to-day."

I learned first-hand what he meant about being on the front lines after my father's stroke and Mom's decline into Alzheimer's. I was thrust into the system, and as painful as it was, I know that my problems are minimal compared to the entire picture of caregiving in the United States. Eight of ten American families will experience or already have experienced a long-term care problem.

The Long-Term Care Campaign's goals are to promote government enactment of a comprehensive long-term care package through a social insurance program that is paid for by all Americans. A program similar to Social Security or Medicare will assure that everyone has access to care.

McConnell believes that the political setbacks that catastrophic coverage and long-term care received in 1989 are only temporary. Demands for services in the future will make those sought after in 1989 seem minimal by comparison.

Epilogue

DEAR HAILA,

Seems funny writing 1990. But it's kind of exciting, too. I'm looking forward to the year 2000. I guess I'm bantering around with small talk because I haven't yet written the words, "My dad died." He died last Thursday, the day you called and left a message on my answering machine.

Making arrangements for the funeral has been a piece of cake compared to getting through the system while my dad was alive. The funeral home has been super helpful and the people at my parent's church have just taken over. This is where ritual enters in—symbols and mythology—and they are important for our survival. They really do help us understand our place in the world. That must be why it's so much easier now.

It's too bad that we haven't developed rituals for dealing with people as death approaches. I don't mean like last rites or an impending death, but when it might be months or even years as in the case of my mom. That type of death is still in the problem stage.

Daddy started going downhill fast by Sunday. His doctor advised me when I was at the nursing home Monday to write a letter saying that I wanted no extraordinary measures used, since he knew that was the wish of my sister and I. Well, I did just that.

I wasn't prepared for Daddy, though. I walked into the room, saw him hooked up to the IV and oxygen, held his hand, looked into his eyes and started bawling. It was so hard to see my dad, who was playing the drums in the band only a few months before, reduced to such a bony mass. I had to leave the room. I walked out and began talking to one of the nurses—a male nurse—Paul. He talked to me for about half an hour and was probably the best source of help I've found so far in coping with all this.

Anyway, while I was driving home, Dad apparently took a turn for the worse and was transported to the hospital—allegedly to Circle City Hospital where his health insurance plan sends patients. Later, I found out the ambulance had taken him to Riverside Community Hospital instead. My sister called and found out that the nursing facility hadn't sent the hospital the papers stating that my father was to have no extraordinary measures. My sister called the hospital and they set up a three-way conference so there would be a witness to her verbal orders not to give extraordinary measures. Once my dad's health insurance found out where he was, they sent him to Circle City, so we had to sign new papers there stating no extraordinary measures.

Before I got the call on Daddy, we had been at my parents' for a few days starting to get things in order for a yard sale and taking care of business. I knew it was only a matter of time until he died, but I had to drive home because of an impending snow storm up here. When I got home, there was a message on my answering machine saying he had died.

My sister took care of the arrangements for the funeral the next day and I did some of the calling from here. Daddy will have a simple memorial service at their church. Then, he'll be cremated and the mortuary will hold the body until we get things straightened out with the Veterans Administration so he can be buried at the memorial park there in Riverside. We couldn't find the papers proving he's a veteran so I've had to send off to Washington to have the main offices send us his records.

I swear to the gods, it's been a hassle from start to finish and it isn't going to let up even with his death. We're in the process now of getting a conservatorship for Mom, and that means a court appearance and the whole thing.

Also, the state Medi-Cal nurse who checks on patients in nursing homes, walked into Orange Tree where my mom is and determined that my mother doesn't need skilled-nursing care—that she should be in a board-and-care home. The nurse has no knowledge that my mom has already slashed her wrists, continues to threaten suicide, can't remember that her husband is dead, and has wandered from the nursing home on at least two occasions. The nurse is saying, without even having the facts, that my mom doesn't need constant supervision. The thing is, when you're with my mom for a short period of time, she carries on a conversation like any normal person. It's like one of the regular nurses said in the nursing home, "Your mother's case is very deceiving. At first you don't even recognize that anything is wrong with her."

So, the attorney will call for a hearing when we get the orders to take her out of that facility, and we'll have to show by her records that she needs constant supervision. There just seems to be no end to this dying.

Truthfully, I can say that never have I felt so old as when dealing with the care of my parents, whether it was trying to get them care at home, placing them into a nursing facility, obtaining a lawyer, or going through the belongings in their home. Sometimes, it seemed like an invasion of their privacy. I not only felt old, I felt like a traitor.

The day I drove down to the center of Los Angeles to meet with the attorney, I glanced at myself in a storefront window and wondered who that old bag was. I looked so awful—harried, tired, beat up, uncomfortable. So I walked into a beauty shop and asked if they had any cancellations. A Chinese guy asked how I wanted it cut. I said I didn't know. Just anything that would make me feel better about myself. He asked why I was in Los Angeles and when I explained about my parents and seeing an attorney, he couldn't do enough for me. I left feeling like a human being again. You know me, I seldom go to a beauty shop —cut my own hair and all that—but it was worth every blessed dollar.

I really appreciate the letters and funny cards you've been sending. Not everyone understands the macabre sense of humor you can develop in the face of death. You're smart to take care of matters now—setting up a living trust and letting your wishes be known legally about how things are to be handled while you're dying and after you die.

The thing is, we hear so many people say it, and we've said it too, "I just want to die in my sleep. That's the only way to go." Well, it isn't the only way to go. Very few people have the privilege of dying like that, even with the hospice movement. Sure, my wishes for my dad would have been for him to receive care at home like we started out to do and for him to die with his family surrounding his bedside. But you can't always have what you want.

I don't feel guilty about most of it because I did everything I could. In the end, you have to shrug your shoulders and say, 'I did my best.' I'm sorry he had to die being shuffled from place to place, but it's kind of like life. If everything went perfect, it would be quite boring.

I've had conversations with people who cared for their parents years ago and have never gotten over some of their guilt, sadness, confusion and bitterness. Some are still at odds with other family members ten years after the death of a parent. One woman told me that she wished she had understood her mother's dementia. She remembers her mom putting underpants on top of her head. She cried about her bizarre behavior and never understood it. She felt guilt that she couldn't care for her mother at that stage. Never mind that she had small children of her own at the time and that other family members had tried and given up.

The night I heard my dad had died, I put on an unmarked video I'd found at my parents home. I had no idea what it was. Well, it was of my dad playing in the band last year at Christmas for a group of people. It was a "home video," so to speak. Most of it showed people's feet and butts as they danced across the ballroom, but every once in a while, the camera zoomed in on the band and there was my little old daddy in his tuxedo and red tie, banging away on those drums. He was so happy and that's how I want to remember him.

I was talking to my neighbors last night about death. The guy was in special forces in Vietnam, so he's dealt with death. We agreed that a sense of humor is one of the few things that will pull you through. I told him about how my son had taken a joke book to the nursing facility and shouted out the jokes to my dad who laughed his head off. I mean, the guy couldn't move, was hooked up to a catheter, knew he was dying, was in a tacky old hospital gown, had this crazy lady living with him in this putzy little bleak room, and he was laughing his head off.

I know time will soften my anger at the system, but I'll still keep on fighting it because that's my nature. I don't want others to have to go through all this. It's tough enough to lose your parents, but when you've got to fight the system while you're doing it, it becomes very unfunny. It's like I told my sister: "I know they're going to lose Daddy's body or something."

Now, we'll start concentrating on Mama. I've gone through her closets and picked out clothing that she'll be able to use over the years. Alzheimer's patients can last forever and it doesn't get very pretty.

I met a woman the other night who is caring for her mother-in-law who is in the first stages of Alzheimer's. She's just beginning to be aware that she and her husband might not be able to continue the care of his mother forever. The husband isn't as worried as his wife. He goes off to work and doesn't realize what is really going on. I hope they're able to handle it before it starts affecting their own marriage. She doesn't know where to start turning for help.

It seems like only the other day that Daddy had his first stroke, but it was nearly three months ago. It's gone from autumn to winter. I've seen the leaves fall and then snow. We had our first real snow the day Dad died. It's so gorgeous. The whole town has turned into a lighted wonderland, what with the snow and the Christmas lights. People up here really go all out for Christmas. No one could get in or out for awhile, so it was just soft, quiet snow falling, and it seemed to help settle my nerves. People came outside all bundled up and threw snowballs and sledded and built snowmen. It was lots of fun.

I still walk about five miles a day. Now I put on boots and walk in the snow back up in the hills. I try to stick to areas where I can see others have walked or where I remember going earlier, but I still got a little lost today. The woods just don't look the same all covered in snow and I couldn't find my landmarks.

The wind is howling outside right now and we're getting ready for another storm. I just love it. It's so odd up here, though. Once it's through storming, the sun comes out right away. Big Bear is supposed to have more sunny days than any place in the state. Also, because it's so dry all the time, it makes for great snow for skiing— the powdery stuff. I'm going to take up cross-country skiing. When I was out walking back up in the hills the other day after the first snowfall, I met a group of cross-country skiers from Canada. Looks like lots of fun and I'm ready for a little of that. I've given up on happy. It's an arcane word at best.

Well, I guess I've blathered along about enough. The holidays sort of cut into my writing assignments. Lots of people are gone so I'm unable to interview them. I'll remember that next year and just take off two weeks. I've spent a lot of time putting things away and straightening up my files, etc. All this happened with my parents right after I moved in here and I've never really had a chance to get things in order.

I'm really looking forward to 1990. I have the feeling it's going to be a great year. I hope it is for you too.

Love, Rita.

Resources

National Organizations Concerned with Health Care and Elder Care

American Association of Retired Persons (AARP), 1909 K Street N.W., Washington, DC 20049. (202) 872-4700. *Provides information on choosing types of care. For list of brochures, write Fulfillment, Box 2240, Lakewood, CA 90802. AARP also coordinates "Healthy US," a campaign of political and consumer action and health promotion activities.*

American Hospital Association Division of Ambulatory Care and Health Promotion Services, 840 North Lake Shore Drive, Chicago, IL 60611. (312) 280-6000. *Serves as a clearinghouse of information on hospital sponsored programs including home care, hospice, primary care and preventive services.*

Children of Aging Parents, 2761 Trenton Road, Levittown, PA 19056. (215) 945-6900.
Offers information on selecting care.

Connecticut Community Care, Inc., 719 Middle Street, Bristol, CT 06010. (203) 589-6226.
A state-licensed, private, non-profit agency that administers statewide programs which enable the elderly to stay at home.

Family Service America, 333 Seventh Avenue, New York, NY 10001. (212) 967-2740.
Will provide information on social service agencies in your area.

Foundation for Hospice and Home Care, 519 C Street NW, Washington, DC 20002. (202) 547-6586.
Research and consumer advocacy.

Health Insurance Association of America, 1025 Connecticut Avenue, N.W., Washington, DC 20036. (202) 223-7780.
This is a trade organization, but they also provide free informative booklets on health insurance. Ask for the Public Affairs Department, or call their Consumer Helpline at (800) 942-4242.

Long-Term Care Campaign, 1334 G St. NW, Suite 300, Washington, DC 20005. (202) 628-3030 or 737-6340.
An umbrella group of 127 organizations dedicated to enacting comprehensive legislation to protect American families against the devastating costs of long-term care.

National Alzheimer's Association, 70 East Lake Street, Suite 600, Chicago, IL 60601. (800) 621-0379 or (312) 853-3060.
Provides information on a variety of resources and programs for those caring for Alzheimer's patients.

National Association of Area Agencies on Aging, 600 Maryland Avenue SW, Washington, DC 20024. (202) 484-7520. *Will provide you with the address of your local "area agency on aging."*

National Association of Home Care, 519 C Street NW, Washington, DC 20002. (202) 547-7424.
A non-profit trade association primarily involved in lobbying on legislative issues relating to home-health care. Also publishes some informational pamphlets—send legal size self-addressed, stamped envelope for a free brochure.

National Association of Private Geriatric Care Managers, 1315 Talbott Tower, Dayton, OH 45402. (513) 222-2621.
Provides referrals to care managers throughout the United States.

National Council on the Aging, 600 Maryland Avenue SW, West Wing 100, Washington, DC 20024. (202) 479-1200.
*Provides information and resources on caregiving and long-term care. Write for a list of their publications. You can contact the **National Institute on Adult Day Care** at the same address.*

National Federation of Interfaith Volunteer Caregivers, Inc., 105 Mary's Ave., Kingston, NY 12401. (914) 331-1198.
Provides transportation, minimal in-home help, and visiting services to elderly as well as referrals to other relevant community services.

National Hospice Organization, 1901 N. Moore Street, Suite 901, Arlington, VA 22209. (703) 243-5900.
Call their Hospice Helpline at (800) 658-8898 for information and referrals.

National Shared Housing Resource Center (NSHRC), 6344 Greene St., Philadelphia, PA 19144. (215) 848-1220.
Information and referrals.

Older Women's League (OWL), 730 11th Street N.W., Suite 300, Washington, DC 20001, (202) 783-6686.
A national grass-roots advocacy organization concerned with issues of importance to midlife and older women.

Senior Service Corporation, 354 Nod Hill Road, Wilton, CT 06897. (203) 834-1644.
Public corporation that provides products and services for elders.

Visiting Nurse Association of America, (800) 426-2547. *This national trade association can provide referrals to home health agencies in your area.*

Supportive Services for Older Adults

Independence Plus
Arkansas Dept. of Health
4816 W. Markham Street
Little Rock, AR 72205-3867
(501) 661-2256

Independence Plus
Kennebec Valley Regional
Health Agency
8 Highwood Street
Waterville, ME 04901
(207) 873-1127

Self Care
Michigan Home Health Care
955 E. Commerce Drive
Traverse City, MI 49864
(616) 943-312

Senior Partners
Visiting Nurse Assoc. of
North Shore & Visiting
Nurse Assoc. of Greater Lynn
85 Constitution Lane
Danvers, MA 01923
(508) 774-9968

Senior Support Services
VNS Affiliates
400 N. 34th
Seattle, WA 98103
(206) 548-8100

Service Consortium for Older Persons
Visiting Nurse Association of
the Inland Counties
1960 Chicago Avenue
Suite D-20
Riverside, CA 92517
(714) 370-2480

Services for Independent Living
1084 Madison Avenue
Albany, NY 12208
(518) 489-4756

United Senior Care
South Carolina
Department of Health and
Environmental Control
3 South Park Circle
Charleston, SC 29407
(803) 724-5841

VNA Independence Plus
Visiting Nurse Association
of Texas
8200 Brook River Drive
Suite 200 N.
Dallas, TX 75247-4016
(214) 689-0009

V.N.A. of Delaware
One Read's Way
New Castle Corp. Commons
New Castle, DE 19720
(302) 382-8200

Your Senior Connection
MCOSS Foundation
67 Main Street
Manasquan, NJ 08736
(201) 223-6200

State Units on Aging

Alabama
Commission on Aging
State Capitol
Montgomery, AL 36130
(205) 261-5743

Alaska
State Agency on Aging
Pouch C, M.S. 0209
Juneau, AK 99811
(907) 465-3250

Arizona
Aging and Adult Admin.
P.O. Box 6123
1400 W. Washington Street
Phoenix, AZ 85005
(602) 255-4448

Arkansas
**Arkansas State
Office on Aging**
Donaghey Bldg., Suite 1428
7th & Main Streets
Little Rock, AR 72201
(501) 682-2441

California
Department on Aging
Health and Welfare Agency
1600 K Street
Sacramento, CA 95814
(916) 322-5290

Colorado
Aging and Adult Services
Dept. of Social Services
1575 Sherman Street, 10th
Floor, Denver, CO 80203
(303) 866-5913

Connecticut
Connecticut Dept. on Aging
175 Main Street
Hartford, CT 06106
(203) 566-7725

Delaware
Delaware Division on Aging
1901 N. Dupont Highway
New Castle, DE 19720
(301) 421-6791

District of Columbia
D.C. Office on Aging
1424 K Street N.W., 2nd Fl.
Washington, DC 20005
(202) 724-5622

Florida
Program Office of Aging
Department of Health
1317 Winewood Boulevard
Tallahassee, FL 32301
(904) 488-8922

Georgia
Office of Aging
Dept. of Human Resources
878 Peachtree Street N.E.
Room 632
Atlanta, GA 30309
(404) 894-5333

Hawaii
Executive Office on Aging
Office of the Governor
335 Merchant Street, Rm 241
Honolulu, HI 96813
(808) 548-2593

Idaho
Idaho Office on Aging
Statehouse, Room 114
Boise, ID 83720
(208) 334-3833

Illinois
Illinois Dept. on Aging
421 E. Capitol
Springfield, IL 62701
(217) 785-2870

Indiana
**Indiana Dept. on Aging and
Community Services**
115 N. Pennsylvania Street
Indianapolis, IN 46204
(317) 232-7020

Iowa
Iowa Commission on Aging
326 Jewett Building
914 Grand Avenue
Des Moines, IA 50319
(515) 281-5187

Kansas
Kansas Dept. on Aging
610 W. 10th
Topeka, KS 66612
(913) 296-4986

Kentucky
Division of Aging Services
Bureau of Social Services
275 E. Main Street, 6-W
Frankfort, KY 40621
(502) 564-6930

Louisiana
Office of Elderly Affairs
P.O. Box 80374
Capitol Station
Baton Rouge, LA 70898
(504) 925-1700

Maine
Bureau of Maine's Elderly
State House, Station 11
Augusta, ME 04333
(207) 289-2561

Maryland
Maryland Office on Aging
301 W. Preston Street
Baltimore, MD 21201-2374
(301) 225-1100

Massachusetts
Department of Elder Affairs
38 Chauncy Street
Boston, MA 02111
(617) 727-7751

Michigan
**Office of Services
to the Aging**
Box 30026
Lansing, MI 48909
(517) 373-8230

Minnesota
Board on Aging
204 Metro Square Building
7th & Robert Streets
St. Paul, MN 55101
(612) 296-2770

Mississippi
**Mississippi Council
on Aging**
301 W. Pearl Street
Jackson, MS 39203-3092
(601) 949-2070

Missouri
Office of Aging
Dept. of Social Services
P.O. Box 1337
Jefferson City, MO 65101
(314) 751-3082

Montana
Dept. of Family Services
P.O. Box 8005
Helena, MT 59604
(406) 449-5900

Nebraska
Department on Aging
P.O. Box 95044
301 Centennial Mall South
Lincoln, NE 68509
(402) 471-2306

Nevada
Division for Aging Services
505 E. King Street, Rm. 600
KinKead Building
Carson City, NV 89710
(702) 885-4210

New Hampshire
Elderly and Adult Services
6 Hazen Drive
Concord, NH 03301
(603) 271-4680

New Jersey
**Department of Community
Affairs**, CN 807
S. Broad and Front Streets
Trenton, NJ 08625
(609) 292-4833

New Mexico
State Agency on Aging
LaVilla Rivera Building
224 E. Palace Avenue
Santa Fe, NM 87501
(505) 827-7640

New York
Office for the Aging
Agency Building #2
Empire State Plaza
Albany, NY 12223
(518) 474-4425

North Carolina
Division on Aging
Dept. of Human Resources
1985 Umstead Drive
Raleigh, NC 27603
(919) 733-3983

North Dakota
State Agency on Aging
Dept. of Human Services
State Capitol Building
Bismarck, ND 58505
(701) 224-2577

Ohio
Commission on Aging
50 W. Broad Street
Columbus, OH 43215
(614) 466-5500

Oklahoma
Special Unit on Aging
P.O. Box 25352
Oklahoma City, OK 73125
(405) 521-2281

Oregon
Senior Services Division
Human Resources Dept.
Rm. 313, Public Service Bldg.
Salem, OR 97310
(503) 378-4728

Pennsylvania
Pennsylvania Dept. of Aging
231 State Street
Harrisburg, PA 17101
(717) 783-1550

Rhode Island
**Rhode Island Department of
Elderly Affairs**
79 Washington Street
Providence, RI 02903
(401) 277-2858

South Carolina
Commission on Aging
Suite B-500
400 Arbor Lake Drive
Columbia, SC 29223
(803) 758-0210

South Dakota
**Office of Adult Services
and Aging**
700 N. Illinois
Pierre, SD 57501
(605) 773-3656

Tennessee
Commission on Aging
706 Church Street, Suite 201
Nashville, TN 37219
(615) 741-2056

Texas
Texas Department of Aging
P.O. Box 12786
Capitol Station
Austin, TX 78741
(512) 444-2727

Utah
Aging and Adult Services
120 North-200 West
Salt Lake City, UT 84145
(801) 538-3910

Vermont
Vermont Office on Aging
103 S. Main Street
Waterbury, VT 05676
(802) 241-2400

Virginia
Office on Aging, 10th Floor
700 E. Franklin Street
Richmond, VA 23219
(804) 225-2271

Washington
**Bureau of Aging and Adult
Services**, OB-44A
Olympia, WA 98504
(206) 753-2502

West Virginia
Commission on Aging
State Capitol
Charleston, WV 25305
(304) 348-3317

Wisconsin
**Department of Health
and Social Services**
1 West Wilston Street
Room 686
Madison, WI 53702
(608) 266-2536

Wyoming
**Wyoming Commission
on Aging**
Hathaway Building
Room 139
Cheyenne, WY 82002
(307) 777-7986

Agencies Monitoring Adult Day Care

Alabama
Dept. of Human Resources
Office of Contracts and
Grants, 64 N. Union Street
Montgomery, AL 36130

Alaska
Older Alaskans Commission
Dept. of Administration
Pouch C, M.S. 0209
Juneau, AK 99811

Arizona
Dept. of Economic Security
Block Grants Administration
Box 6123, Site Code 086Z
Phoenix, AZ 85005, *or*

Dept. of Health Services
Office of Long-Term Care
411 N. 24th Street
Birch Hall
Phoenix, AZ 85008

Arkansas
Arkansas Office on Aging
Donaghey Building, Ste. 1428
7th & Main Streets
Little Rock, AR 72201; *or*

Office of Long-Term Care
P.O. Box 1437
Little Rock, AR 72201

California
Department of Aging
Adult Day Health-Care
714 P Street, #378
Sacramento, CA 95814; *or*

Dept. of Social Services
Community Care Licensing
Division, 744 P Street
Sacramento, CA 95814

Colorado
Dept. of Social Services
1575 Sherman Street
Denver, CO 80203; *or*

Colorado Health Dept.
Facility Regulation Division
4210 E. 11th Avenue
Denver, CO 80220

Connecticut
Connecticut Dept. on Aging
175 Main Street
Hartford, CT 06106

Delaware
Delaware Division on Aging
1901 N. Dupont Highway
New Castle, DE 19720; *or*

**Delaware Division
of Public Health**
Jesse S. Cooper Building
Dover, DE 19901

District of Columbia
D.C. Office on Aging
1424 K Street, N.W., 2nd Fl.
Washington, DC 20005

Florida
**Aging and Adult Services
Program Office**
1317 Winewood Boulevard
Building 2, Room 328
Tallahassee, FL 32301; *or*

Medicaid Program Office
1317 Winewood Boulevard
Building 6
Tallahassee, FL 32301

Georgia
Office of Aging
878 Peachtree Street, N.E.
Atlanta, GA 30309

Hawaii
**Department of Social
Services and Housing**
P.O. Box 339
Honolulu, HI 96809

Idaho
**Bureau of Licensing and
Certification**
Dept. of Health and Welfare
420 W. Washington Street
Boise, ID 83720

Illinois
Illinois Dept. on Aging
Long-Term Care Division
421 E. Capitol
Springfield, IL 62701

Indiana
**Indiana Dept. on Aging
and Community Services**
115 N. Pennsylvania Street
Indianapolis, IN 46204

Iowa
Iowa Commission on Aging
326 Jewett Building
914 Grand Avenue
Des Moines, IA 50319

Kansas
Kansas Dept. on Aging
610 W. 10th
Topeka, KS 66612

Kentucky
Cabinet for Human Resource
Dept. for Social Services
Division of Aging Services
275 E. Main Street, 6-W
Frankfort, KY 40621; *or*

**Licensing and Regulation
Office of the Inspector
General,** Cabinet for Human
Resources, same address.

Louisiana
Office of Family Security
P.O. Box 44065
Baton Rouge, LA 70804

Maine
Bureau of Maine's Elderly
State House, Station 11
Augusta, ME 04333

Maryland
**Department of Health and
Mental Hygiene**
201 W. Preston Street
Room 305A
Baltimore, MD 21201; *or*

Maryland Office on Aging
301 W. Preston Street
Baltimore, MD 21201-2374

Massachusetts
Dept. of Public Welfare
600 Washington, Room 740
Boston, MA 02111

Michigan
**Office of Services
to the Aging**
Box 30026
Lansing, MI 48909

Minnesota
**Minnesota Department of
Human Services**
Centennial Office Building
4th Floor
St. Paul, MN 55155

Mississippi
**Mississippi Council
on Aging**
301 W. Pearl Street
Jackson, MS 39203-3092

Missouri
Missouri Division of Aging
Broadway State Office Bldg.
P.O. Box 1337
Jefferson City, MO 65102

Montana
Adult and Aging Services
Management Operations
Bureau, Box 4210
Helena, MT 59601

Nebraska
Dept. of Social Services
P.O. Box 95026
Lincoln, NE 68509

Nevada
Division for Aging Services
State Mail Room
Las Vegas, NV 89158

New Hampshire
**Department of Health and
Human Services**
Hazen Drive
Concord, NH 03301

New Jersey
**Div. of Medical Assistance
and Health Services**
324 E. State Street, CN712
Trenton, NJ 08625

New Mexico
Human Services Dept.
Adult Services Bureau
P.O. Box 2348
Santa Fe, NM 87501

New York
State Office on Aging
Agency Building #2
Empire State Plaza
Albany, NY 12223; *or*

State Department of Health
Division of Health Facilities
Standards and Control
Bureau of Long-Term Care
Corning Tower
Empire State Plaza
Albany, NY 12237

North Carolina
Division of Social Services
325 North Salisbury Street
Raleigh, NC 27611

North Dakota
Aging Services Division
State Capitol
Bismarck, ND 58505

Ohio
Ohio Department of Aging
50 W. Broad Street
Columbus, OH 43215

Oklahoma
Division of Aging Services
Dept. of Human Services
312 Northeast 28th Street
Oklahoma City, OK 73015

Oregon
Dept. of Human Resources
Senior Services Division
313 Public Service Building
Salem, OR 97310

Pennsylvania
Pennsylvania Dept. of Aging
Division of Program Mgmnt.
231 State Street
Harrisburg, PA 17101

Rhode Island
Dept. of Elderly Affairs
79 Washington Street
Providence, RI 02903

South Carolina
Dept. of Social Services
1520 Confederate Avenue
Columbia, SC 29202-9988

South Dakota
Dept. of Social Services
Adult Services and Aging
700 N. Illinois
Pierre, SD 57501

Tennessee
Dept. of Human Services
111-19 7th Avenue N.
Nashville, TN 37211

Texas
Dept. of Human Services
Office of Services to Aged
and Disabled, P.O. Box 701
701 W. 51st Street
Austin, TX 78769

Utah
**Utah State Division of
Aging and Adult Services**
150 W. North Temple, # 326
Salt Lake City, UT 84103

Vermont
Vermont Office on Aging
Agency of Human Services
103 S. Main Street
Waterbury, VT 05676

Virginia
**Virginia Department of
Social Services**
8007 Discovery Drive
Richmond, VA 23288

Washington
**Department of Social and
Health Service**
Bureau of Aging
Office Building 43-G
Olympia, WA 98507

West Virginia
**West Virginia Department
of Human Services**
Adult Services
1900 Washington Street
Charleston, WV 25305

Wisconsin
Wisconsin Office on Aging
1 West Wilston Street
P.O. Box 7851
Madison, WI 53707

Wyoming
**Wyoming Commission
on Aging**
Hathaway Building
Cheyenne, WY 82002

The Pepper Commission on Comprehensive Health Care

This commission was established in 1988 to produce recommendations to Congress on access to long-term care and acute health care for all age groups.

Commission members from the senate are:
> **Max Baucus** (D-MT)
> **Dave Durenberger** (R-MN)
> **John Heinz** (R-PA)
> **Edward Kennedy** (D-MA)
> **David Pryor** (D-AR)
> **Jay Rockefeller** (D-WV)

Members from the House of Representatives are:
> **Bill Gradison** (R-OH)
> **Mary Rose Oakar** (D-OH)
> **Pete Stark** (D-CA)
> **Tom Tauke** (R-IA)
> **Harry Waxman** (D-CA)
> **Louis Stokes** (D-OH).

Other members include **James Davis**, president of the American Medical Association; **James Balog**, chairman of Lambert-Brussels Capital Corporation; and **John Cogan** of the Hoover Institution at Stanford University. Chairman of the commission is **Jay Rockefeller**.

If you wish to present your views to the Commission, they can be contacted at (202) 225-9950, or by letter at Room 140, Cannon House Office Building, Washington, DC 20515.

Self-Help Clearinghouses

These clearinghouses can help you find a free support
group for caregivers in your area.

National

Self-Help Clearinghouse	(201) 625-7101
Self-Help Center	(312) 328-0470
National Clearinghouse	(212) 642-2944

By State

California	(800) 222-LINK
Connecticut	(203) 789-7645
Illinois	(800) 322-MASH
Kansas	(316) 686-1205
Massachusetts	(413) 545-2313
Michigan	(800) 752-5858
Minnesota	(612) 642-4060
Missouri	(816) 361-5007
Nebraska	(402) 476-9668
New Jersey	(800) FOR-MASH
New York	(518) 474-6293
Oregon	(503) 222-5555
Pennsylvania	(412) 247-5400
South Carolina	(803) 791-2426
Texas	(214) 871-2420
Vermont	(800) 442-5356

Suggested Reading List

Books

Eighty-Five Plus—The Oldest Old, Beverly Sanborn, Wadsworth Publishing.

Living in a Nursing Home, Sarah Greene Burger and Martha D'Erasmo, Ballantine.

Making Peace With Your Parents, Harold H. Bloomfield, M.D., Random House.

Outreach With the Elderly, New York University Press.

Parentcare: A Common Sense Guide for Adult Children, Lissy Jarvik, M.D. and Gary Small, M.D., Crown Publishers.

When Your Parents Grow Old, Florence D. Shelley, Harper & Row.

Where Do We Come From? What Are We? Where Are We Going?, The Gerontological Society of America. To order, write: The Gerontological Society of America, Department 5018, Washington, DC 20061-5018.

Other Reading Materials

The Caring Home Booklet, can be ordered through the Program in Policy and Services Research, Andrus Gerontology Center, University of Southern California, Los Angeles, CA 90089-0191.

Consumer Notes: Help for the Working Caregiver, American Council of Life Insurance/Health Insurance Association of America, Company Services, 1001 Pennsylvania Ave., N.W., Washington, DC 20004-2599.

Home Evaluation Checklist for the Elderly, and *Home Evaluation Resource Booklet for the Elderly* can be ordered from Birch, Davis & Assoc., ASSIST, 8905 Fairview Road, #300, Silver Springs, MD 20910.

Independent Living (Magazine), 44 Broadway, New York, NY 10016.

About the Author

RITA ROBINSON is the winner of 22 journalism awards and a member of the American Medical Writers Association.

Her other books include the widely acclaimed *Survivors of Suicide* and *The Palm: A Guide to Your Hidden Potential*.

She lives in the mountain community of Big Bear City, where she is currently at work on a book about the joy of being single.

ORDER FORM

☐ **PLEASE SEND ME A FREE CATALOG.**

Name_____

Address_____

City_____State_____Zip_____

Quantity	Book Title	Unit Price	Total
	Being Human in the Face of Death *edited by Deborah Roth, MSC & Emily LeVier, MSC*	$9.95	
	Stepping Stones to Grief Recovery *edited by Deborah Roth, MSC* *The Center for Help in Time of Loss*	8.95	
	Gifts for the Living: Conversations with Caregivers on Death and Dying *by BettyClare Moffatt, MA*	9.95	
	The New Age Handbook on Death & Dying *by Rev. Carol W. Parrish-Harra*	9.95	
	Survivors of Suicide *by Rita Robinson*	9.95	
	When Your Parents Need You: A Caregiver's Guide *by Rita Robinson*	9.95	
	AIDS: A Self-Care Manual (Third Edition) *by AIDS Project Los Angeles*	14.95	
	The Law of Mind in Action *by Dr. Fenwicke Lindsay Holmes*	10.95	
	The Laws of Wealth *by Dr. Fenwicke Lindsay Holmes*	10.95	
		Subtotal	
		Sales Tax 6.5% (Calif. only)	
		Shipping/Handling ($2.00 per book)	
		Total Due	

Send Check or Money Order to:

IBS PRESS
744 Pier Avenue
Santa Monica, CA 90405
(213) 450-6485

IBS PRESS
744 Pier Avenue
Santa Monica, CA 90405